FAR

Also by Victoria Lancelotta

Here in the World: Thirteen Stories

FAR

A NOVEL

VICTORIA LANCELOTTA

COUNTERPOINT

A MEMBER OF THE PERSEUS BOOKS GROUP

NEW YORK

Published by Counterpoint,
A Member of the Perseus Books Group.
All rights reserved. Printed in the United States of America.
No part of this book may be reproduced in any manner
whatsoever without written permission except in the case of
brief quotations embodied in critical articles and reviews. For
information, address Counterpoint, 387 Park Avenue South,
New York, NY 10016-8810.

Counterpoint books are available at special discounts for bulk
purchases in the United States by corporations, institutions,
and other organizations. For more information, please contact
the Special Markets Department at the Perseus Books Group,
11 Cambridge Center, Cambridge, MA 02142,
or call (617) 252-5298, (800) 255-1514
or e-mail j.mccrary@perseusbooks.com.

This book is a work of fiction. Names, characters, places, and
incidents either are products of the author's imagination or are
used fictitiously. Any resemblance to actual events or persons,
living or dead, is entirely coincidental.

Library of Congress Cataloging-in-Publication Data
Lancelotta, Victoria, 1969-
Far / Victoria Lancelotta.
p. cm.
ISBN 1-58243-114-0
1. Italian American families—Fiction. 2. Italian American
women—Fiction. 3. Baltimore (Md.)—Fiction. 4. Single
women—Fiction. I. Title.
PS3562.A4669F37 2003
813'.6—dc21   2003004758

Text design by Cynthia Young; Set in 12.5 Perpetua

03   04   05 / 10   9   8   7   6   5   4   3   2   1

ACKNOWLEDGMENTS

*My abiding thanks
to Noah Lukeman, tireless champion, fighter of the good fight,
and Dawn Seferian, sweet voice of reason, sanity, and kindness.*

FAR

BEFORE WHAT IT WAS ENDED, before I moved away, before he met my sister, her husband and I were ugly together.

On a good night, I could match him drink for drink and reach beneath the table to his lap before the room started to spin. On a good night, he drove us back to his apartment and opened a bottle of wine long after it was necessary, long after my shoes were off and my stockings run and my hair damp on my forehead.

We never went to dinner, or to movies, or for walks along the harbor. We never saw one another on Saturday afternoons unless they had bled from Friday nights, blinds low, ashtrays spilling over, wine dried in red granules at the bottom of glasses and our eyes burning with brief sleep and exhaustion. We never ate together, but my sister's husband scraped me raw.

———

I went from work to a bar downtown where the bartender had tattooed hands and I sat at a table in the back of the room. I ordered a glass of wine and watched the door, girls with metal through their lips and crimson hair, torn pants low on their hips and pint glasses, and the bouncer on his stool, shaved head and cell phone.

I felt forgotten, and ready, polished shoes and stockings and bare thighs above. The floor was planked, uneven, scarred wood and splinters, and I imagined my heels digging into the shoulders of Edward's suit. I drank my wine and ordered another, and the bouncer snaked out an arm to draw a girl into his lap. She leaned in to whisper, her hand cupping his scalp, then slid down and walked past me on her way to the pay phone, a thin strip of leather knotted around her neck, wire tangles of earrings, her hair a halo glow. Her face was clean, smooth and pale, and she turned on her way to speak to the bartender, words I couldn't hear, and he nodded and laughed, and I faced the front of the room again and Edward was walking toward me, watching her. He came to the table and threw a pack of cigarettes down.

"Do you need a drink?" he said.

"I already ordered one. How are you?"

"I'll get it," he said, and glanced toward the bar. "What was it?"

"Cabernet." I pulled a cigarette from the pack, slid it back in. "Get two of whatever you're drinking. I've been here for a while."

He went to the bar and came back with three glasses, hands circled around them, and leaned over the table to put them down, a small clatter, no spills. He sat at an angle from me, his right side facing slightly in toward my left so that our sight lines would have met, if they were to meet, at the door, so that any-

one walking in and seeing us would imagine we were both wait-
ing for someone else.

Let me be clear. I wanted nothing from him, or nothing that I
could have explained to anyone who would have asked, sympa-
thetic, wondering at how I could drag through my days and
nights alone while my friends got married and bought houses
and pictures for their walls, tasteful frames, sideboards. I was
not unhappy, and I was ashamed to tell people this. I left my bed-
room windows open at night and I didn't cry.

The girl came back from the pay phone and stopped at the bar.
She anchored one foot on the rail by the floor and leaned over on
her arms, her shirt pulling up and away from the waist of her
pants, her back, a crescent of flesh like a smile. We watched her.

"What are your plans tonight?" I said. This was how it went. I
assumed nothing past the initial phone call, the drinks in front of
us. We would play through these things, brief talk, eyes averted,
and if he suggested another round I would begin to drink more
quickly, a race to tie.

He kept his eyes on the girl's back, and the bartender drew
her a beer.

"Don't know. Finishing this drink," he said, and turned to me,
shook a cigarette from his pack. He smiled. "My plans tonight
are to forget today."

He sold houses. He would meet my sister in a bar like this
one.

We finished our drinks and he got up for more and the room
filled, tall unsmiling boys with long hair. In another drink I would
move my chair enough to let my leg touch his, jukebox feeding
out distortion and standards, the little girls hard and bright like
gemstones. In another drink he would cup my elbow in his hand
and squeeze—drink faster—and we would speak at one another,
words running fast and meaningless, incidental to teeth and lips.

I could say that these nights bruised me, or cut; opened be-
neath my skin to silence, but that is not the truth. I could say
these nights didn't fill me, but they did.

There were no empty tables left, and once it was dark enough
the bouncer propped the door open with his stool and girls
shouted down the steps to the street, pretty girls, white skin,
tattoos curling around arms, around necks, and Frank Sinatra
sang to them.

Edward leaned into my hair, perfume under smoke, and pre-
tended to tell me stories. He was thirty-five years old then, and
waiting for nothing. I didn't know his politics or ethnicity. I
knew that he was a vegetarian, that he had a younger sister. We
talked about our younger sisters. I knew that he preferred sleep-
ing alone and that in his sleep he would turn into my back and
slide an arm down my side and a foot over mine, and that when
he woke he would not have liked for me to tell him he had done
this. I knew what kind of shampoo he used and that his towels
were monogrammed.

His voice in my ear: "I took these people to look at a house and
the lawn wasn't mowed, the lock was stuck, I had to take them
in through the garage with these piles of shit, newspapers every-
where and dog carriers, and inside it was—"

I was thirty years old. I lived in an apartment on the second
floor of a row house in the city, a front door and vestibule and
another door, a different key for each, and the narrow wooden
steps that led up into my living room, a rectangle, kitchen at one
end and bedroom at the other. I mailed my rent check on the
twenty-third of each month. My landlord was a Middle Eastern
man who owned an ice cream shop. He offered me free pints of
pistachio and fudge ripple. I took my clothes to the Laundromat
down the street and ate pistachio or fudge ripple, and across
from me in a plastic chair an old woman would sit, cotton dress,

white ankle socks, a plastic knitting bag at her feet and inside a transistor radio, newspapers, a baseball pennant, a naked doll and a change purse. The two of us watched the dryers spin.

"They hadn't even cleaned the refrigerator, there were clothes on the floor of the laundry room. I talked to them yesterday, for Christ's sake, we set the appointment up."

His hand moved up from my knee to my thigh, a cilice, and his fingers kneaded the fabric of my skirt, rubbed it against bare skin. I drained the wine from my glass and tapped it against his, a cheap bell, his ice cubes melted and swirling pale into scotch. I turned my face to his moving lips, red and wet. He was lovely, his face angular, fine lines tracing his mouth, still moving. I imagined myself more beautiful than I was, a reflection of him.

The night after this, a friend of mine would be beaten, a call after midnight. I would wake and dress and drive, forget to turn my headlights on until another car flashed brights at me and the driver yelled from the open window. The streets were empty, air blowing warm, slippery, and the hospital white, too clean to hold me, I was dry, dry. This friend was alone in her room. She was neither black nor blue, she was yellow and rose, the colors of a sunset, a quilt.

But this night we were still in the bar, and nothing was decided.

"Do you want to stay here or go someplace else?" I said to him. The ashtray was full, his pack a crumpled ball of cellophane on the wet table. The legs of our chairs were crossed beneath it and when I closed my eyes I saw a small sky, veined and starred. His jacket was draped over the back of his chair and his cheek was at my neck, his face turned out to the blue and swirling room, and the girls were dancing together, arms above their heads like ribbons. He spoke against skin.

"Do you want to know what I tell people about you? I tell them you'll do anything I say."

Decide, I thought. The truth was that he asked nothing of me. I was silent, waiting. He pushed his chair back and reached into his pocket for cash.

"Where's your car?" he said. He counted out a stack of bills and I saw the bartender watching us. "He's been looking at you all night," he said, smoothing the money flat in his hand. "I know him," he said, and smiled.

"I would bet a lot of people know him."

"Would you?" he said. He lifted his jacket from the back of the chair and shrugged into it, smiling, his lips almost blue in the hazy light—"Any other bets, Martha? As long as you're in a gambling mood?" His face was flushed, his eyes narrow. "Would you like to place odds on what you're going to do for me when we leave here?" He leaned over the table toward me, hands flat between empty glasses, his back almost horizontal in a stretch, the pose of an angry woman.

"No," I said. Ten minutes earlier he had been wrapped around me, his breath soft in my hair, and I had been thinking of him in sleep, smooth skin, his arm warm on my hip.

"Pull around in front and wait for me. I have to settle up."

I did this. I picked up my coat and purse and moved through the girls at the front of the room, nodded to the bouncer. The air outside was cold and I walked fast down the block and around the corner, keys in my hand. Across the street a girl walked in the opposite direction, a man following close behind, speaking softly. He turned and saw me watching.

"Almost there, baby. You wait," he said.

It was a night in early April, neither the beginning nor the end, and hours later I would wake before dawn to see the bathroom door closed, a line of light beneath it, and hear sounds that were either sobs or laughter, choking, tight, water running uselessly. I would straighten the sheets and wait.

I got into my car and locked the doors. In my rearview I saw the girl across the street turn the corner in the direction from which I had just come, the man still following, no closer than before.

I drove to the front of the bar, left the car running and turned the hazards on. I could see Edward in the doorway, his hand on the bouncer's shoulder, leaning in to listen, to laugh. The girl I'd seen on the street ducked past them, into the heat, and there was a pounding by the side of my face, the car rocked sideways; the man who'd been following her beat on the glass with the flat of his hand—"Open the fucking window, I can smell you, open it baby, suck you up baby, you smell like money bitch—"

My foot jerked off the brake and the car lurched forward. He took quick steps to keep up, shouting, his face inches from mine and I pressed on the horn and the girls on the steps of the bar turned, bottles to lips; Edward behind them, watching, a cigarette burning between his fingers, the bouncer's skull a cold moon and Edward's face a star above it, his teeth, his pretty mouth laughing.

———

I lived on the top floor. Across the street from my door was a liquor store and bar, the houses on either side of it boarded up. I circled the block and parked in the only space I could find, around the corner by an alley, church on one side and post office on the other.

I told myself, when I lived there, that the neighborhood was safe, that the street was lit and trafficked, buses ran often; that families still lived there, children still chalked the sidewalks after school and in summer. These things were true, but when I came home at night I walked quickly, key chain in my fist and the longest key out, tight between index and middle fingers.

The door to the bar was open and I could see a piece of the room, the backs of men and the mirror along the wall, my own house blurry in it. I unlocked my door and waited behind it.

I was tired, drunk by more than half and leaning against the door, watching for Edward's headlights. I imagined my parents, who lived less than a mile from where I stood: my mother in bed, eyes closed, her face blue in the flickering light of the muted television, and my father at the kitchen table two flights down, newspaper spread in front of him and a glass of iced tea, something I never remembered him drinking when I—he— was younger. The tea was something new for him, and he bought boxes of it, herbal, blended, stacked in the pantry like a child's blocks, paler colors. He worried over it at the stove, steeping and straining it into clean glass jars. Mornings in the summer he sat the jars on the back stoop outside the kitchen in a sliver of early sun. Coming to the back door, I saw these be- fore anything.

When I saw Edward crossing the street I unlocked the door, opened it and stepped back into the narrow vestibule, and it seemed to me that his face had changed, darkened under his eyes and around his mouth. It was not even eleven o'clock.

"Did you bring your friend?" he said, and snaked an arm around my waist.

"What?"

"Your friend. From the car," he said, his dark mouth moving above me. It was cold in the open doorway and his hands were warm, soft through my coat. I imagined them covered in fur, brown and sleek. They moved down my coat and below it.

"Close the door," he said. "I thought you might've given him a ride somewhere. Do you two go way back?" He walked me back, his leg forward between mine, and I pushed the door closed behind him.

"Can you lock it for me?" I said. "Turn the bolt."

Sable, mink, the length of my back, the tops of my legs and the choke of pearls I didn't have.

"The lock," I said.

"Peace wanted to know where I got you," his warm hand on my throat. *Piece?* I thought. "The bartender," he said—had I spoken? His hand kneaded my throat. My ankles hit the lip of the bottom step; sixteen steps to the top and another door, to my apartment, my floor, standing open, heat radiating from there.

In another house my mother slept on her own top floor, in that dry heat, and my father slept below her, the vertical path twisting down through stair railings, through years, and a cup of tea at the bottom, newsprint on the tablecloth, silence; and in another house across the city a friend slept next to the man who would crack her jaw, a few ribs, not too many, just enough. I stepped back and up and he followed, smiling, his quick hands in front of him, dropping pearls.

My bedroom was bright, the streetlights almost level with the windows. When I think of this now the bed seems wider than it was, is, this bed I still sleep in in another place; the sheets a pale tangle and his body whiter than that.

If I had loved him I would have kissed his forehead, his fingertips, each one a small gift and perfect. "Tell me what to do," he said, and if I had loved him I would have answered. I would have said *Build me into something, put me together piece by piece, make me into something that wants, that needs—Do. This.* Glass broke below us on the sidewalk, the street, and I lay beneath him, still and listening. Downstairs a dog barked, scratched; the door to the hallway below us opened, and the front door. I didn't know my neighbors' names and I was still, and above me his face fell away and beneath it was bare want, and beneath my own skin was a cool space, slow and silent.

Outside, the street flashed blue, red, and sirens sang over the barking dog, doors opened up and down the block—what had I missed?—and he moved above me, eyes closed. *Believe nothing you can't see*, I thought. My father, not far, would have heard from another direction.

I thought of that girl, her hair, her white skin, in the doorway of the bar—still there?—shivers raising her thin arms above her head, dancing for the room; and I thought of my sister, pretty college girl, a sweater and scuffed boots in a house in Delaware with a plastic cup of beer, chewed rim, and up the stairs from where she stood closed doors on either side of a hallway, carpet damp and brown and fraying. Door number one, door number two, door number three—two girls fighting, voices lowered even though no one in the house would hear, would care; five people sitting solemn on the floor, cigarette butts in empty Coke cans, a pipe passed gently; her roommate, pants off, eyes glazed, a boy with a baseball hat and torn jeans *Do you need me to get you another drink?* And my sister with her plastic cup, no reason to worry for tomorrow or the next day, imagining that this was nothing, a quick stop on the way to someplace better.

Before dawn in silence, the street gray, his smooth face in sleep, too still; the stools in the bar upside down on high round tables, damp towels hanging over the lip of the well. I reached for a cigarette on the windowsill. There were no matches and the candles had burned out. My sister alone on top of her covers, shoes off, the other bed empty. This was how I wanted her to be. Little girls, smeared lipstick on pillowcases, jewelry tangled on dressers, bright earrings twisted over lobes, forgotten; and my father after the long climb, newspaper ink smeared into a damp pajama sleeve, a story, a part of one. I leaned on the sill and behind me he turned and drew the blanket up in sleep, the curl of fingers over the edge in that high small room, floating. All your little girls, Daddy, tucked into nothing. This was where I lived and breathed.

THIS IS HOW TO SAY GOOD-BYE.

The first thing to go is the hair—before, Edward wrapped it around his fist, held it like a drowning man, but it was my chin that came up to suck for air. Alone in the shower it spread over my back, heavy with water, and I wound it into a twist like licorice. That same twist will be snicked away, secured with elastic at both ends and brought home from the salon, put into the back of the top dresser drawer. It will lose all human scent.

The next thing is to eat, or not eat, depending.

I am thin, so thin. A day or three without eating much of anything besides carrots, or some chips, and the body closes up, refuses anything more. Hunger stops, becomes nausea and subsides, then nerves thrum, live wires. And to start again is hell, bare feet to flame—a little at a time, a small salad, a piece of bread, butter if you can, gently, gently.

But in the meantime, in the process, the bread alone will do, soft pieces a few times a day and fruit, green grapes cold from the refrigerator bin. A handful of grapes, coffee until five P.M. and wine from then on. This is enough for what I am doing: emptying closets, drawers, neat piles of clothes on the bed and floors. Ruthless—plastic bags filled with faded shirts, blood-stained underwear, worn socks and sweaters with fraying sleeves. What's salvageable goes folded into brown handled bags, to the Salvation Army truck, handed up the steps to a man with a clipboard. *No receipt, thank you,* but I will be watching the street outside my window for the next few days to look for some thin woman in black pants, or a green silk dress, worn once to a wedding, a small spot of champagne by the left shoulder. Sandalwood, faint, fading.

Next, cleaning, floorboards scrubbed with vinegar and water, doorknobs polished, bleach in the sinks. The fumes come up and burn my eyes white. A bowl of rice in a clean kitchen, a few drops of sesame oil. The bowl sits half-empty on the counter, evidence of effort, and the windows are open, incense in every room, high sweet smoke.

The magazines are stacked, the refrigerator empty, my hair dark on its folded cushion. These rooms could be floating over nothing.

And after all this, in the clean dark quiet, bathe. Scalding water and steam on tile, a sponge that smells of hyacinth. I set a glass of wine on the back of the toilet and strip, throw my clothes on top of used tissues and cotton balls in the small trash basket, and in the water time around me is slow, heavy and solid. I slide low into the heat, and everything is possible. I imagine the echo of these rooms, empty, or the sound of them filling with someone else's boxes, rolled carpets propped against walls, lengths of wrinkled tape fast to the dusty floor. Someone will open kitchen drawers and closets, blindly feeling shelves above her head for a piece of something left behind, finding nothing.

I knelt on this floor and poured water from my hands on his shoulders, down his back. Candles threw long shadows on the walls and flicked his skin with fire and I soaped and dried him, reaching up as he stood to press the towel to his face, his neck, to press the heat out. In the bedroom, on the sheets, on my skin he was damp. The ceiling was white and wide and I closed my eyes, opened them again and waited.

This was months ago, and there were clothes on the floor and empty glasses, a bottle of wine on the night stand; July through the open window and the fan moving July through the room, through my skin, and the heat of his voice in my mouth. I remember the sound of a pipe on the street outside, the end-to-end flip, hollow clang of metal on asphalt and high laughter fading, but inside, silence, his lips moving underwater, his eyes floating open and blind.

But now, remember, bathe. Outside it is dry and cold. Scrub and rinse, scented oils, step out of the tub and dry in the air, no towel, skin marbling on the way to the bare empty bedroom and the bare empty body is an offering, sweet, fragile; touch it and it dissolves like cotton candy, pink sugar.

In July he reached for the bottle on the night stand and held it to my mouth, balanced the curved base on his long lovely fingers and tilted it up until it ran warm, faster than I could drink it ran down my chin and when the bottle was empty it fell to the sheets and he cradled my head with his hand, with the barest tips of those five long fingers while the rest of him punched into me like hail.

July, July, July—my mother's birthday, *What do you want Mommy?*

I want you to be good then

I want you to be happy then

Nothing and the years ran on.

But now, dry, and no matter what, the hands stay to the side, away. They don't touch the body, they don't even think of it, don't think at all, stupid bits of flesh—wrap them in cellophane, stamp, label and date them and put them on a refrigerated shelf where they can't hurt anyone. They don't want, no part of me wants, and of course this is a lie. My mother sleeps in a blue nightgown in the blue light of the TV while my father nods silently two floors down and my sister clutches a fat yellow high-lighting pen in her hand while the boy across the library table from her looks on with miserable hope and my friends polish their dining room tables and lie down on them to fuck with a sense of purpose that I've never had.

What I want is to look at them and understand how presence is enough. The phone sits on the bare floor, wrapped in its cord, umbilical. My parents have been married for over thirty years and their silence is axiomatic, neither amicable nor hostile, muted snow on the screen. What I want is to crawl inside of it and listen. I lie down on my bed, bottom sheet and blanket, one pillow. The phone sits useless, lovely and white. My mother used to clean every day, one room at a time. There was a schedule: top floor to bottom, Monday to Saturday. Every morning, furni-ture polish, vacuum, rags and feather duster, bucket, a sponge pad to kneel on for scouring floors. Summers I cleaned next to her, slippery lemon smell. I asked for years why we couldn't take a day to do the whole house, one day, long hours but free until the next week, wouldn't that be easier? Wouldn't that make more sense? *This is the way we do it.* Period. And I didn't understand the simple reason, the filling of part of each day like water in a glass. Cleaning till eleven, maybe noon. A bath, then she tore and rinsed the lettuce for dinner, pounded meat, dredged it in egg and flour and breadcrumbs, steamed vegetables. Four o'-clock: *Martha. Set the table.* Empty hours between four and six and I stayed far from her. I took Carly into the backyard and we dug in the dirt with spoons. Every day—cleaning, cooking, dishes and sweeping after dinner, by eight the glass full and ready to be poured down the drain and set upside down on the dish rack. Bed. A friend of my father's sold Fuller brushes and he came home from work one night with a sponge mop. It had a lever on the handle you could pull to squeeze it almost dry—no wet hands, no kneeling. *Look how easy, Ann.* She would not use it.

What I want is to crawl in bed beside my mother and listen for my father's breathing two floors down. What I want is to spread my days open on the floor and see noise and motion and me in the middle, small and bright. What I want is a steak, cool red inside. What I want is a cigarette.

I clean this apartment on my hands and knees and when I finish I am sticky with dust and sweat—nothing inside me but my skin is a magnet. You'd pray for something like that. This is how to say good-bye: empty everything. My bags are in the vestibule, my car is filled with gas, and I am going to drive as far as love goes.

My PARENTS AND I WERE ON their front porch under an October gray sky, my father in an awful sweater and new jeans, my mother in a housecoat. It was eight A.M.

"Did you get the car checked out?" my father said. The jeans were carefully creased and newly hemmed, the thread at his ankles too brightly orange.

"I did. Tires, oil, fluids, the whole bit. You're not supposed to iron those, Daddy." I pinched the stiff fabric between my fingers and my mother grabbed my hand.

"I want you to call tonight when you stop," she said. "It doesn't matter what time, we'll be up, but don't stop too late. I don't want you driving too late."

"You won't be up. If I called at six you'd be sleeping."

"I'll be awake. And I mean it, I don't want you to exhaust yourself. And stay at a nice motel. Make sure you get a second-floor room." She let my hand go and put her arms around my neck, cold flannel sleeves.

"Okay," I said. "Inside with you, it's cold out here. Go. Daddy," I said, and held my arms out. He pressed a folded bill into my hand.

"Drive safe. You have the AAA card? Goddamn thing better be good for something."

His cheek was rough and red. He smelled of tea with milk. "Get rid of that sweater, huh? You should wear blue. Your eyes," I said, and he let me go. I thought *I don't want your money,* and I put the bill into my pocket.

"Work starts Monday," I said. "I'll call you with the number." My car was parked behind me, a bag of pretzels on the seat and a large coffee sitting on the hood. It would be cold by the time I drank it.

"Call," my mother said. There was a white spot in the sky where the sun would have been.

"If you talk to Carly today tell her I'll call her in a few days."

And I waited, imagined the small television on in their kitchen and the bowls of grapefruit halves and cereal on the table, the coffeepot and teakettle. My father put his arm over my mother's shoulder and she stepped forward slightly, kicking at the broken neck of a bottle in the grass, and out of his reach.

As fast as that.

———

I didn't drive straight to the interstate. I balanced my coffee between my legs and drove through the city to Edward's house. It was a porch-front, wider than my parents'; he shared it with two other men. It was almost nine and his car was not on the street. I parked and took my coffee with me to the front door. The curtain didn't quite cover the window and I angled myself to look through: newspapers piled on the floor by the couch, empty wine glasses on the coffee table, the television on. On the screen were two people sitting in chairs on a stage, crying. I rested my hand on the front door and imagined a low vibration, the feel of a house waiting.

On the corner down the block were three children, bright corduroy pants and open coats, their books and lunchboxes in a pile by the curb. The girls spun around the bus stop signpost like hands on a clock, one ducking under the other, and the boy, smaller, grabbed at the backs of their jackets as they whirled past him, screaming *Bitch! Bitch!*

You ain't nothin, ain't no one!

There were pens and paper in my car. I could fold a sheet and press it into the doorjamb, by the knob. *I came by but you were gone already.*

I'll call you from the road.

Just drive south, take a right when you get to Florida.

Please forgive me.

I'm not sorry.

The boy lunged like a stray dog, grabbed at a sneakered foot. She leapt away with such grace, her legs like ribbons and her coat ballooning behind her, and the other girl, close on her heels, reached down just as gracefully to slap the boy, her palm catching the back of his head.

I blew into the lid opening of the cup out of reflex and drank. A bus pulled to the curb, brakes whining, and the girls bent to collect books and lunches, taking up the boy's as well as their own. They crowded behind him as he stepped from the curb, looking right and left for traffic, their hands on his back.

I poured the coffee out onto the brown grass and walked back to my car, opened the door and sifted through the maps and folders on the floor until I found a sheet of clean paper. It would take so little, it would take almost nothing—a few lines, one, less than a minute, less than an explanation but enough. I was digging through the glove box for a pen when someone tapped the window.

"Martha. Hey, what's going on?" It was Reid, one of Edward's housemates. I'd met him a few times, late at night or early in the morning, and I'd always felt a sense of shame and told myself it was because of my smeared makeup or knotted hair. Edward had rocked me on the bed in his room, murmuring *Sweet girl, sweet angel,* and when I closed his door behind me in the morning and went down the stairs with my shoes in my hand, so quiet, Reid would be on the sofa with a cigarette—*Hey, what's going on?*— and I felt as though my skin were evaporating, dissolving into so much white smoke and floating away from me.

I rolled the window down. "Hi, Reid. I'm just—"

"You taking off?" He was wearing a long tweed coat, sleeves cuffed. The lining was pale yellow and satiny. He held a steaming cup of coffee and a lit cigarette in one hand.

"Moving," I said. "Heading out now, actually."

"Uh-huh, uh-huh. Edward's not here. He left before I got up. Is that everything?"

"The furniture got picked up yesterday."

"Uh-huh. Yeah," he said, and smiled, wide and bright and not a little vacant. His teeth were perfect. "You going for good?"

"I don't know. My boss is opening a new store and I'm getting it started."

"Well hey, good luck then." He took a drag off the cigarette and flicked it into the gutter, shivered and stepped back. He was wearing a striped pajama top under the coat. "Listen," he said, "did you want to leave anything for him?"

Sweet girl. He'd threaded my hair between his fingers and touched the tips of his thumbs to my temples, rubbing small circles. In bars he snaked his hand under my shirt and forced it up, laughing.

"No. Reid, would you mind not saying—" and his smile then was not vacant at all.

"How about if you were gone before I saw you?"

The sheet of paper was still resting in my lap and I found myself returning his smile, mine neither as wide nor as perfect but genuine all the same, and for a moment I was ready to cry.

"That would be great. Thank you."

"Okay then. You were never here." He leaned down and rested his arms on the edge of the door. I could smell the coffee. "Are you planning on calling him? Because he's, you know—"

"What? What is he? Angry, miserable, none of the above? Because I couldn't tell you." I was shaking my head, folding the paper into a small accordion. My voice was louder than it needed to be. "I have no idea. I don't know if he thinks this is some kind of joke or punishment for something or a point, if he thinks I'm trying to make some kind of point—"

"Martha. Hey. You're asking the wrong person. You're . . . shit. Forget it. I don't even know what I was going to say." He straightened up and looked down the street toward the bus stop. There was a woman on the bench with a clear vinyl bag on the ground by her feet. Her hair was a brilliant orange, her socks white and folded around her ankles.

"I don't even know why he was with you. And I don't mean that like it sounds. But Eddie—man, don't ask me what he wants."

"Okay. Look, I need to get moving. Maybe I'll see you sometime."

"Uh-huh. Take care," he said, and turned up the walk to the porch, and already I believed him, believed that we had never seen each other, never spoken at all.

I pulled out onto the street, drove slowly to the corner and stopped. There were no cars behind me. "Ma'am? Excuse me?" I shouted from the open window and the woman at the bus stop reached immediately for the vinyl bag. "I could give you a ride if you're not going far."

Her eyes were a violent blue, narrow and pouchy. She looked at me with not suspicion so much as contempt: unreasonable, stupid, but right.

"Get the fuck away from me," she said. "You think I don't know about people like you? Fucking pervert! *Dyke!*"

I did not move until I heard a horn honking behind me, and even as I drove forward and turned the corner, the woman stared after me, grinning, her lower lip collapsed against bare gums.

———

What will happen eventually is this: Edward will marry my sister. She will come home from college for Christmas and do her best to occupy the space in the house that both of us had filled until then. She will lie on the bed and watch ice skating specials on the television while our mother sleeps next to her. She will bake cookies and bring cartons of eggnog home from the small grocery store on the corner. They will sour on the refrigerator shelf. She will wrap garland around the railings of the stairways and call me after dinners, handing the phone to our mother and father in turn, and when they give the phone back to her to say good-bye her voice will be small.

When it seems to her that she can no longer breathe she will take the car and go to meet her friends at a bar on Thames Street. They will line themselves in a row with Irish coffees steaming in front of them, shots of whiskey on the side, and count off the days, the hours, until it is time for them to pack their bags and return to their schools. They will watch cartoon

Christmas specials on the small television over the bar and talk themselves into believing that they are happy to be where they are. When Edward walks in he will sit down next to her and drape his overcoat on the back of his stool. He will notice her hair and the way she tucks it behind her ear. He will notice the ear, the small silver hoop strung through with a piece of turquoise. He will motion to the bartender to get her another drink and when it appears in front of her she will turn, surprised and pleased, and see an unexpected gift.

But how this happens does not matter. This or something like it will happen a hundred times over, a thousand, in bars up and down Thames Street in the week before Christmas, when people imagine that the tightness they feel in their chests is neither desperation nor despair but excitement, hope and good faith, and it will never be any less heartbreaking for that.

She will thank him and drink her drink, and her friends will nudge her and giggle to one another. She will agree to meet him again, and on Christmas night, after the wrappings have been thrown away and the bows put back into a shopping bag for another year, and another; after the glasses have been rinsed and dried and our parents put to sleep on the bed and the sofa, she will drive to Thames Street and have no trouble finding a parking spot. He will already be sitting at the bar. It will matter to her that there is an Irish coffee waiting, and it will also matter that when he asks about her family, her life, he will seem to do so not out of obligation but genuine interest. This, of course, will be true. And when she tells him about her sister, he will give no indication of knowing me.

Around them the room will fill slowly, faces reflecting red and gold and green from the blinking lights. The bartender will wish each person a Merry Christmas as she hands over beer and whiskey, and very few will respond in kind. Edward will reach into a pocket and draw out a small white box and place it on the bar, and behind him voices will be raised, a woman will sob—*Why didn't you tell me?*—and the man across the table from her will pry her hands from her glass and bring them to his lips but she will snatch them away and hold them in her lap like injured animals. My sister will open the box—delicate drops of garnet and silver—and in her eyes Edward will spin into the brightest star.

The couple at the table behind them will leave the bar and walk along the water, down to the end of the pier, where they will stand wrapped in scarves and sweaters and try to form words. They will tell each other that their lips and tongues are stupid and slow because of the cold and decide to walk the short blocks to their house, and when they find that the silence has followed them there they will tell each other that it's because of the drinks they've had. They will take their mutinous bodies silently to bed.

On Thames Street the lights will sparkle and glaze the sidewalks into ribbons of candy. People will leave large tips on their tables, grateful; another Christmas will have been got through. Edward will walk my sister to her car, hold the door for her and pull the seat belt over her shoulder. He will promise to call her. He will.

In the white and silver glow of the new year, she will call and tell me what he does to her. I will close my eyes and listen, memory twisted up and soaked with July, warm red wine and the sounds of a kickball game in the alley behind my house and his hands opening me up into something larger than myself. My sister's voice will sing through the wires and I will hear myself asking *What else? What then?* as though we are teenagers again and wishing for that, for the big dark room over the kitchen with the open window and the two beds on either side of it, for flowered nightgowns and pink-painted toes. I will tell myself that what I am hiding from her is inconsequential, a scratch on the skin that will leave no mark. I will tell myself that this, too, does not matter. And she will sing and sing.

My FATHER GOES VISITING. Every other afternoon he drives to the hospital to sit with an old friend who will not be able to leave to die. His friend is on a wing that is a sort of residential facility; the common room there has photographs of the patients on the walls, posed group shots and candid ones so that it is possible for two people to sit at a table and play cards under a framed picture of themselves playing cards.

My father's friend does not play cards. He lies in his bed and my father turns the television on when he goes to see him, turns the channel to a ball game or the news and speaks as though he is understood. This man never married and has no family; one day the nurse on duty called my father to tell him that his friend was not in his bed, not anywhere on the ward. When he arrived at the hospital his friend was back in his room, wrapped in blankets and sitting in the chair. A woman had come in to the emergency room, the nurse told my father, to say that there was an elderly man wearing a cotton gown and paper slippers walking slowly down the street in front of the hospital. Orderlies had gone to bring him back. My father screamed at the nurse and his friend sat motionless, staring into the middle distance.

After he leaves the hospital he drives to his widowed sister-in-law's house and lets himself in with his key. He sits with her at the dining room table to drink instant coffee and eat homemade cake. In her dining room, on the sideboard, are photographs of my father and his older brother, black and white, creased beneath the glass, the two of them in jeans (dungarees, my father still calls them), their hair high in front and slick. Cigarettes burn between their fingers; they squint against an old sun. My aunt's cakes are sweet, dark brown and crusty on the bottom. When my father's friends and family die he goes to the funerals. He does not visit the graves.

On my parents' own sideboard is a picture of my mother kneeling in a plastic wading pool on the strip of grass in the narrow back yard of the house where Carly and I were born, where my parents still live. My mother holds my sister in her lap, small feet, heels digging into tanned legs, fat hands held out and balanced in narrow ones. My mother's hair is teased, silver-blond and almost translucent. Her lips are frosted, pursed the minute before a smile.

My sister cut herself the day that picture was taken, stalking a bird on hands and knees to the edge of the grass and beyond to the paved walkway, the latched gate to the alley behind the yard. She slapped her hands down flat to find a shard of glass, bottle-green and pretty in her palm. She waited until the blood began to rise before crying and our mother caught her up, carried her inside and iced her hand, held tweezers to a match, and operated.

My father's sister-in-law wears crocheted bedroom slippers and short white socks. She brings bottles of Amaretto and Sambuca and a tiny stemmed glass, vines burned white around the rim, and begs him to drink—*Please, Joseph, just a little with the cake. It's so dry without.* She watches him drink and eat and they talk, they tell stories that hold no surprises for either one of them, that neither has forgotten, but in the telling the dead speak.

When my father finishes he takes his dishes to the kitchen. He checks the burners on the stove, the water heater, the thermostat; puts the milk back into the refrigerator and sniffs for spoiled food. He makes sure she does not see him do these things. He bends to kiss her on the cheek before he leaves, and she squeezes his shoulders as hard as she can. Her fingers are knotted, fragile as candles.

———

The night my sister cut her hand our father and I went to a carnival. I dressed in denim shorts and a halter top, pulled my hair up through the vent of a baseball cap. Our mother lay on the sofa in our basement, TV on, fan turned high, with my sister asleep on top of her, the bottom of her bathing suit damp with sweat. I leaned in to kiss my mother good-bye and she took my face between her hands, drew it away from her.

"Is that makeup I see?" she said, turning my face to the light.

"Just lip gloss. What you got me for my birthday."

"Nothing else?" She let my face go and shifted Carly against her. "Okay. You guys behave yourselves. And bring me back some fried dough."

Nothing else. My lips were shiny and faintly pink, and I pressed them together often as my father and I walked the seven blocks to the carnival. Our church was at the corner of the avenue and a one-way cross street; bright yellow sawhorses blocked the traffic. We stepped into the crowd. There was a wooden booth on the sidewalk, a woman inside, her hair curled tight, wheels of red paper tickets unwinding on the shelf at her chest: for the Ferris wheel, the pony rides, for chances to win the wire-strung stuffed animals and hanging plants in the stalls.

"Joey! Joey!" she called, waving at my father. Her arm jiggled wildly. We walked over to her, my father smiling and reaching into his pocket to pull out a handful of crumpled bills.

"How are you, Therese?" She leaned out to kiss him. "Taking in much money tonight?"

"Not so much from the kids. Sunday's our big day—how are you, baby doll?"

"Fine," I said, and took a step away from them to look past the booth and deeper into the crowd. The streetlights were on but the lights strung across the tops of the stalls burned brighter to me, tiny halos around each one if I squinted. There were people I recognized from church and many more I didn't and for a moment I felt cheated—I wished that I had asked my father to let me come alone.

"How many tickets you want, hon?" Therese asked my father, and he smoothed a bill on the ledge.

"This'll work for now. We might come back for more later."

She slid the money into a metal tray under the ledge and unwound the tickets. "Take a few extra. You give every Sunday," she said, and winked. "Where's Ann and the little one?"

"They're staying home tonight. They'll probably come over tomorrow afternoon."

"I won't be here, so you tell them hello from me. My daughter's coming to pick me up tomorrow. I'm going to see the grandkids." She waved to me and I smiled. My lips were going dry and I ran my tongue over them, barely, barely, and my father tore off a length of tickets and said, "What first? The Ferris wheel?"

"Could we just walk around a little first?"

There was not far to walk. The length of the carnival was just over a short side block, intersected at the midpoint by a narrow alley like the one behind our house. But there were people, a hot press of them. Along the sidewalks behind the stalls were families sitting on their front steps, on green-painted metal benches bolted to the concrete or lawn chairs they'd pulled from tiny back yards. Their doors were open and I could see into the front rooms of their houses, plastic-covered ottomans and crocheted blankets draped across the backs of couches. In the street where we walked were couples with small children and groups of boys in cutoffs and unlaced tennis shoes. The boys darted between people, carrying paper soda cups, running backward and spitting ice at one another. I recognized a few.

We turned at the end of the block to walk back toward the lights and my father stopped at a stall for drinks.

"A Coke and a beer," he said, sliding the tickets across the wood.

"No beer, hon," the woman said. "Father Anthony said no beer this year."

My father smiled. There was beer on bingo night, every Thursday. Father Anthony had been to dinner at our house. He was a small man with a narrow smile and long grayish fingers. My mother set his place where she usually sat, across the length of the kitchen table from our father. When she poured his wine he raised his hand before the glass was even half-full, a pantomime repeated endlessly throughout the meal.

"Two Cokes, then." He handed me a cup. "When I was your age the priests made wine in the rectory. Worst stuff I ever tasted."

We stood in line for the Ferris wheel. It was the only ride and the line was long, families three and four abreast with children anchored between their parents, alternately jumping up and down and crying. My father handed the boy working it our tickets and we climbed into the rocking car and waited for the metal bar to be snapped into place. The seats were torn red vinyl.

"When I first met your mother we came here and I took her on this. She was okay till we got to the top and when we started to come down I thought she was going to faint. Her face was green." He laid his arm across my shoulders and I imagined my mother, heart racing at the bottom, and then there was the feel of air rushing beneath me and the creaking of the gears, and I squeezed my eyes closed. The car moved backward and up in a series of jerks, the people below us getting smaller and smaller as they were loaded onto the cars, and we climbed.

"Hold on," my father said, and shifted his weight, hands gripping the safety bar as he rocked the car enough to move us through the still air. I imagined him doing this with my mother, and how she must have had to bite the insides of her cheeks to keep from screaming for him to stop. When my father drove us anywhere my mother sat bolt upright in the front seat, her arms straight ahead of her, hands gripping the curve of the dashboard. She hadn't learned to drive until after they were married.

"Look, Martha," he said, and we were level with the roof of the church. I turned in the seat to look over it and the street-lights below stretched on in neat rows. I could see down the avenue to our house and past, to the place where traffic merged onto Monument Street, four lanes wide and curving along the Jewish graveyard and the string of used-car lots beyond. I could see the stadium, the ring of lights a bright circle, and thought that if I had the nerve to stand I would be able to see the players on the field, hear the crack of bats and the cheers of the crowd dissolving into the dark humid sky.

When the cars had all been loaded and locked the boy at the controls switched gears and the wheel began to turn, fast enough to feel the suck and swoop of air around us and too fast to see, to focus on a roof or light or park, a square of green dark crisscrossed by pale winding paths like chalk tracings. My father lifted his arms and whooped as we dropped. The people on the ground shrank and stretched and I waited for the ride to be over, to sit in the car while the boy turned the wheel slowly enough to empty and load it again, for the spread of sky to open up around me and the step of rooftops to drop down to the harbor I could not see. We were close to water.

My father checked his watch when we got off. "You want to take a look at the ponies? Then maybe get the fried dough and head home?"

There were ponies in the alley, five tickets a ride. When we'd come here before Carly was born I'd ridden them, hanging on to the horn of the saddle while an old man led the animal by the reins, a trip up the alley and then back, five, six ponies at a time, some with two children on their backs. I couldn't imagine where the parish got them, or how. They were heavy-headed, their sides round, their shoes echoing sharp on the concrete.

At the mouth of the alley was a small knot of people waiting for the ponies to make their slow way back. There was the smell of fresh manure and under that the smell of trash from a Dumpster cooking in the heat. Boys led the ponies back, boys older than me in jeans and T-shirts or flannel shirts with the sleeves rolled up, fingers hooked on the bridles. Music floated out from farther back in the alley, a portable radio in the narrow dark and the sounds of girls laughing.

"Do you want to get the dough now?" I said.

"No ride?"

"I think I'm too big for them. They don't look too strong."

"They don't, do they?" My father checked his watch again. "Okay. We should probably be heading back anyway. You want to get another soda? I'll split one with you."

We stood in line in the parking lot behind the church. There was a long kitchen in the church basement, the top half of one wall open onto the lot so we could see down inside. Women with aprons and floured hands were lined against fryers, dipping stainless steel baskets filled with hand-sized pieces of dough into boiling oil. The hot smell was heavy around us and we passed the soda back and forth until there was only ice. The pieces came out of the fryers deep gold and the women covered them with powdered sugar and layered napkins between them before sliding them into brown paper bags.

This was twenty years ago. My father's friend still lived in the row house he'd grown up in and went to spaghetti dinners every Friday at the church. He sat at a table with us when we were there, and he and my father played cards after the dishes were cleared away. My father's brother was still alive. I was ten years old—I had never flown in an airplane, but when I finally did I thought of the Ferris wheel, the rooftops and thrum of lit sky.

My father and I sucked ice from the cup and moved through the line, and behind us girls sat on the hoods of cars at the far end of the lot, smoking cigarettes and spraying perfume from small bottles they pulled from peeling imitation-leather purses. They combed their hair and drummed their heels against the grilles and boys stood around them in raggedy half-circles. I remember thinking that the girls looked like they were getting ready for something, but it seemed to me then that everything that could happen to them that night was already happening: frosty pink lips and silver chains glinting against their throats, woven rope bracelets and wooden-soled sandals. They were perfect in themselves. I imagined that if I stood close enough to them the smell of frying dough would dissipate in a haze of lemon and baby powder.

They drank from paper cups and when they'd tipped them up and empty they handed them back into the cars for their friends in the seats to return them, magically full again, passed carefully from one to the next by fingers around the rims, the paper buckling soft in the heat. Anything they want, I thought, with no idea what else there could be to want, and when the boys leaned in to one another to whisper the girls kicked at their shins, laughing, then shouting when a boy pulled a shoe from a foot and tossed it around the circle before returning it to its owner.

My father handed a length of tickets to the woman at the counter and pocketed the rest. He balanced the bag in the palm of his hand, grease blooming circles on the paper. When we got home Carly would be awake and the four of us would sit around the kitchen table and lick the melted sugar from our fingers.

Behind us a boy slid one of the girls from the hood of a car, his hands circling her waist. She leaned against him, her hair falling over the side of her face, and hooked her fingers through his belt loop. Her smile was dizzy, wide and forgiving, and when we passed them on our way to the street she flung her arm out in laughter and caught my father's shoulder.

"My God, I'm so sorry!" she said, and the boy snaked his arm over hers, drawing it across her chest and taking her hand in both of his. She was stumbling, her ankles turned outward in the thick-soled sandals, but he walked her forward, arms around her and one leg behind, as straight as he could. Her hair was the shade of blond that I would later recognize as the burnt gold of peroxide. It glowed under the lights. She smiled at me and her smell was not lemons but something heavier, closer to the ground.

———

We ate the fried dough in the kitchen, storm door open to the screen, radio tuned to the ball game, the lights. My mother brought Carly in from the couch and sat her on a chair. She chewed at the dough, head propped in her hands, eyes closing.

"I'll take her up tomorrow," my mother said. "They still have those awful ponies?"

"Yeah. Remind me to give you the tickets."

My father had not *taken* me, I remember thinking. We had gone together, brought back food for my mother and Carly, done what was asked of us.

Three years later I went to the carnival with two friends and we bought sodas, walked back and forth along the block too many times to count, each of us pretending that there was something new and wonderful to see, something we'd missed on the last pass. We bought sodas and sat on the curb in back of the church, and if a boy we were watching looked back we turned our heads, checked our watches or got up to throw an empty cup into an overflowing trash can. The year after that I went alone and waited by the alley for twenty minutes—twenty precious minutes, my watch synchronized with the kitchen clock, no excuses for being late—before I felt a hand on my shoulder and turned to see him standing there, half-smiling, smelling of whiskey. He said nothing, just pulled me by the hand around the block and behind the Laundromat. We were alone for fifteen minutes, less, his hair tangled in my fingers and his hands over the back of my shirt, moving down to reach inside the waistband of my jeans. The small of my back, drugstore perfume, Lily of the Valley and bourbon? Scotch? I didn't know. I tasted it on his lips. He smoothed his hair and we walked to the mouth of the alley, not touching. Three of his friends were waiting for him. He pulled the flask from his back pocket and they passed it around, and then he offered it to me and I drank, short sticky neck,

metal and the sweet taste of whatever it was. I took only enough
to swirl in my mouth, nothing to swallow. *I'll see ya*, he said, and
the three of them walked off into the crowd.

In my pocket I had a few dollars, my house key and a lipstick. I
had thought we would get sodas, sit on the church steps that
faced the avenue. It was early, over an hour until I had to be
home. I pulled the lipstick out but I'd forgotten a mirror. The
top of the lipstick was worn down flat, not angled like my
mother's. I swiped it across my bottom lip and used my finger to
paint in the top one.

I bought a Coke and walked the length of the booths, slowly,
pausing to watch women putting quarters down on numbered
squares drawn on the wooden ledges. The wheels spun and peo-
ple clapped, yelled for their numbers to come up, shouted and
cheered when they won a basket of cheese or a fern. I thought I
would buy a few pieces of dough to take home—my parents
wouldn't expect that.

Behind the church the line snaked out into the parking lot.
There were a few cars there, not many, and behind them, in the
far dark corner, he and his friends stood against the wall of the
rectory. There were a few girls with them, the same girls I'd
seen standing across the street from school in the afternoons,
their books stacked on the sidewalk behind them, no book bags
or uniforms. They went to the public school.

I kept walking, past the line for the dough and the parking lot,
fast down the alley as though I hadn't meant to stop at all, had
wanted nothing more than to take a shortcut home. It had been
light when I left the house, and I'd promised my mother I
wouldn't walk home alone. She knew his parents from church.

I walked down the avenue and the closer I got to home the
emptier the sidewalk got until there was no one on it save a
few old men, shorts and socks and sandals or bedroom slippers,

T-shirts, small radios on the steps next to them with the sounds of the ball game across town. There was no way to see the stadium lights from where I was.

I sat on our own front steps. The basement windows were bright—they were downstairs, in the kitchen, waiting for me to come down the back steps and in through that door. They couldn't see me out front. I wondered if he'd seen me walking by, seen my lips frosted and shining again after he'd kissed them clean, seen that I didn't care.

We walked around and he bought me cotton candy and we took a few chances on Mrs. Rinaldi's sauce. He said it's better than his mother's. Have you ever had any? Then we went on the Ferris wheel and he rocked the car really hard and we could see the lights on at the ballpark. What's the score, Daddy? And when we got off we met up with some kids from school and we walked around some more and that was it. I was going to bring back some fried dough but the line was really long. He said he'll call me tomorrow.

I checked my watch. Fifteen minutes. I drank the rest of the Coke—it was all I could taste, that and the waxy peach of the lipstick.

They were sitting at the table, drinking beer and playing cards. The fan was set up in the corner. My mother checked the clock. "Very nice," she said. "Didn't he want to come in?"

"He dropped me off out front."

"Did you have a good time?"

Cotton candy and Mrs. Rinaldi and the Ferris wheel, fried dough, long lines. The words came.

WHEN THEY LOOK AT ME, they see what my face has become but no more than that; they see the years in lines and shadows, the bright long hours. They see the body, the work in progress that in an ironic reversal becomes less perfect each day. They see the smile that still comes quickly, empty more often than not but believable nonetheless.

They see the hands, the blunt polished nails and silver rings. Gold is for women not like me. I am most proud of my hands and feet, vain about them, long fingers and toes, smooth skin. There is nothing I would change about them. They are useful. I wish I could say as much about the rest.

When they are close enough they smell a faint musk, some dark flower, petals curled against skin.

When I was sixteen my mother sat me down on a stool dragged into the bathroom, the round bulbs above the mirror brighter than any other light in the house. She laid a towel over the toilet lid and covered it with jars and brushes and compacts. *You should learn to do this right*, she said, and painted me.

I remember the bells of the ice cream truck, discordant. When I was much younger I was sure there were words to its song, a song the ice cream man sang in the cab of his painted van. My father and Carly ran to meet him and brought back dripping papered sticks and cones, and my mother called downstairs to put ours in the freezer. Her fingers were quick and light on my face.

I looked like a showgirl, eyelids smoky, my lips a bright glossy red, penciled carefully just outside of the edges. *That garbage you wear on your lips makes you look sick. You need some color, Martha. Red is always in style.*

The bathroom smelled of her powder, a circular cardboard container with an oversized puff resting on top of it, ivory and sweet.

When they look at me they start at my face and work their way down, lingering on the places they'll need.

You should get rid of all that makeup you have. It's junk. We'll go shopping.

The cold water in the sink ran tepid. I went down for the ice cream. *Oh my*, my father said, *well*. Carly ran upstairs. *Do me, Mommy! Do me next!*

Some of them, the mannered ones, are careful. They meet my eyes, smile pleasantly and turn their attention elsewhere. They look again only after I have stopped.

In the freezer, my father said. A strawberry shortcake bar, bits of crumb coating sticking to the waxy paper. *You should wash your face*, he said, and winked. At eighteen I looked at them and saw exactly what they knew. No lipstick for them, no high heels or perfume, nothing to wrap themselves in, no ritual. Their bodies, so solid to look at, were fragile, their faces glass, nothing to cover them. They smelled of soap or their mothers' houses, or the beer they bought for six dollars a case. When I looked at them at eighteen I saw my own dizzying reflection.

My mother was married at nineteen, divorced at twenty, a year of her life eaten by someone who has no face or name. In our house was her yearbook photo and then no others until her second wedding, my father's hair dark and slick in the picture. He was not young.

When I look at enough of them their faces become interchangeable.

At fifty my mother was in bed by nine every night, the dishes stacked in the drainer, pots drying on the stove. When I came home the lights were on, the door unlocked, my father asleep on the couch. I came home singing, reeling, a cut on one knee from where I'd tripped climbing out of a car, a burn on my hip from a dropped cigarette. When they looked at me they said *You're beautiful,* they said *You're mine,* they said *Will you let me? Will you let me?* and I looked at them and smiled, laughed, I said *Yes. Yes. Yes.*

My mother said to me *There are things you're too young to understand.*

My father said to me *She's just tired. Don't worry about me. You have enough to worry about.*

I stood swaying over my father's sleeping body, shoes in one hand and the other on the arm of the couch for balance. I whispered to him and imagined in his dreams he would hear my mother's voice inviting him. My own voice was hoarse, my lips tasted of peppermint gum. I sat on the floor and rested my hand on his chest, drank the last of his tea in the glass on the table, wiped my face with a tissue and put fresh lipstick on. He did not wake.

They said *I don't want to lose you,* their lips against the pulse in my throat. We locked ourselves in bathrooms, embroidered hand towels and blue shell soaps. Outside the doors was music, the sound of breaking glass, crying and laughter and music turned louder. The smell of my mother's powder was every-where, my lips bitten raw. I came home singing, falling.

Daddy, how could you let this happen to you?

I sat in church on Sunday mornings between the two of them, Carly on the end of the pew, swinging a foot out into the aisle. My father's rosary looped over his moving fingers, the wooden beads smooth with wear. My mother stared straight ahead, lips moving. The boys huddled at the back of the church by the door, sunglasses on, hands in pockets. I would have to walk through them after the final benediction. Yellow dress, flat shoes, my fa-ther's hand on my back, the warm weight of it. Go in peace. They said *Hi Martha. Hi Mr. Romano,* and my father smiled at them, circles under his eyes, but he smiled as though they were his own sons.

They said *Martha, don't stop. God don't.* I'm sitting in a diner on the main street of this town, men in work pants and heavy boots at the counter, in short-sleeved shirts and ties in the booths. Women spread napkins across their children's shirts and unwrap straws for their drinks. They curve into the seats and around their children, their bodies pliant, existing only in contact with something else.

The sun burns through the glass front wall. A man gets up, pays his check at the register on the counter, leaves a tip on the counter. He jingles change in his hand, or keys. Every time the door swings open I look up. I'm waiting for no one, invisible.

I DON'T WANT YOU TO BE KIND to me *or take care of me. None of that is necessary. All I want is your presence. Your occasional presence. This will be easy.*

This is what I told Edward, over and over again.

I don't want you to tell me where you've been and I don't want you to ask me about my day. Don't offer promises or sympathy or kind words— these things are a waste of your voice. I want you to treat me like a stranger. I want to be a stranger to you for as long as I can.

He didn't know my family, or any of the people in my neighborhood. But I was with him. I was with him. This is what I told myself, over and over again. So much telling for so little, for such a small thing.

I want you to be with me like this.

He was agreeable.

As few words as possible.

His voice was like deep water.

———

"So what's Edward's excuse?" Connie said to me. We were in the kitchen of their new house, making dinner. Her husband Don was at the liquor store. "Why isn't he here? I figured you two would be spending every goddamn minute together."

"He had a late showing. Some house in Essex—he was supposed to show it yesterday but when he got out there the place was a mess, so he had to reschedule." I had no idea whether this was true or not. I hadn't invited him here. We didn't go to other people's houses for dinner, didn't bring bottles of wine or desserts, didn't make polite conversation. It was all we could do to speak to one another, sometimes.

"I don't know, Martha. I just—I don't get it. I can't understand what you're doing with him."

I'd known her all my life, she and her husband both. They'd been married for two years and together for ten. At their wedding reception, Don had wept. He followed me to the bar and when I turned around with a new drink he put his hands on my shoulders, his lips wet and swollen: *I just want you to be happy, Martha. We both do. Connie's so worried about you.* I was there alone. I stood and waited for him to finish speaking.

You're drunk, I said. *Everyone here is happy.*

"This knife is dull," I said. "You're going to slice your hand open if you keep using this."

"What happens when you move?"

"What?"

"With Edward." She turned the flame up under a pan. "Have you two talked about that? Who visits who?"

"Connie, I don't know. Nothing," I said. I put the knife in the sink and reached for another one. "Nothing happens. I go and he stays. That happens."

"Then why did you even start it? What was the point?"

"Why are you so concerned about this?" I said. Color was up in her face and her mouth was tight, lips pressed white. "It has nothing to do with you. You don't even know him, Connie."

"That's exactly my point. I've seen him once, for about ten minutes, in how many months? How many has it been? And your family's never met him and he never goes anywhere with you—"

"Listen to me," I said. I wiped my hands on a towel and took her by the shoulders, spoke slowly, smiled. She was angry with me, I knew that. "We're fine. I'm fine. There's nothing for you to be worried about."

"All right," she said. "Fine. I'm not going to argue with you." She shrugged my hands away. "But it's not right. I'm sorry, it's not."

We don't fight. We don't lie. We are careful to stay in the places we belong even when nothing separates us but a thin slick of sweat. We keep our own counsel. And when we hurt each other it is a deliberate thing, objective, neither messy nor random; nothing for which we would need to apologize. We are neat. Everything we do is ordered, perfect: a house with no one in it.

When we were in school Connie was beautiful, and she had no idea of this. I curled her hair and painted her nails and at parties the boys said *Martha, get Connie over here. We have to ask her something important* and collapsed against one another, laughing. And Don, his shirt clean and ironed but his hair too long, his beautiful hair, said, *Fucking assholes,* and went to get her himself, to walk her out to the backyard or down the block to sit on the church steps. And so it went for months, years; they stayed together

while the rest of us ran through every possibility, every permu-
tation, the ten or so blocks around the parish school in constant
motion, back doors slamming, fathers screaming and mothers
crying, girls hiding in closets, whispering into phones pressed
tight to their ears, boys waiting on corners for whoever would
come to find them. Connie and Don played cards with his par-
ents on Friday nights and went to visit her grandparents after
church on Sundays.

"Get the glasses!" Don yelled, slamming the front door closed
behind him. "The booze has arrived."

―――――

Sit down my mother had said to me. *There's something I need to tell you.*

We were in the kitchen. I was starting college in less than a
month but not moving, not leaving, not yet. That would be for
Carly to do. The laundry basket was on the floor, sheets folded,
my father's shirts lying across the top, and the air was sweet and
warm. The dryer hummed and thumped in the back room.

When I was younger. About your age—

She was wearing a flowered dress, loose but not loose enough.
When I'd crawled up into her lap as a little girl it had never
seemed large enough, her tiny waist, her sleeveless turtleneck
shirts and narrow cropped pants. All that was long over.

I was married, she said. *Before I met your father. Not for long, but I was.*

She was near tears, terrified. She pushed her hands into the
folds of her dress and breathed as though she had climbed some
great height, and I remember feeling disgusted with her, her
quivering chin and wide fingers, cuticles torn and scabbed over. I
was overwhelmed by her flesh, its permanence and gravity. My
mother had been beautiful, and she had choked on it.

*It was less than a year. And when it was over I went home to your
grandparents and lived there until I married your father. He's been want-
ing me to tell you—your father. And it's taken me this long because—*

What happened? I said.

I'm telling you.

No. I mean who was he? Why did you split up? What happened to him? To the two of you?

That's not important. Listen to me. I didn't tell you because—

My nails were ragged. I remember the chipped polish, broken edges. It was late afternoon and I had plans that night. Time, I checked the clock over the oven and my mother saw me do this. I didn't care about the reasons, the intervening years—I'd been there for that.

Because I didn't think you needed to know yet. Because I was worried what you would think of me. Because it really doesn't matter anymore except that I didn't want to lie to you.

And I sat there while she talked, her voice damp, defensive; scraping bits of polish from my nails, eighteen years old, my God, how could she have worried what I thought of her? I didn't think of her at all.

Obviously this is not something you care too much about. Her voice was hurt, full of a dignity I didn't recognize. She pulled a napkin from the holder on the table and wiped her face with it. *That's fine. Just please don't tell your sister.* She stood and picked up the laundry basket, left me sitting there.

I took a shower, blew-dry my hair and set it in hot rollers. I filed my nails and repolished them. I don't remember where I went that night or whom I was with. I remember someone whispering in my ear—*I could fall in love with you*—and shaking my hair back from my face, lighting my cigarette from the tip of someone else's, someone who said to me *Whatever he's saying, you better not believe a word of it, Martha* and thinking I would never be so stupid.

I came home to a sleeping house. My mother had set bowls and spoons out on the counter, ironed my father's shirts and hung them in the alcove by the dryer. My own clean clothes were stacked on my dresser. Her house, her family. The one she had.

Did you believe everything he told you? Would I recognize the words? Did you think you were lucky? Were you lucky for a while? How long was that while? Did you wait for him to come home from work, lipstick on, perfume? Did he shower before dinner, try to pull you in with him, your curls drooping in the spray? Did you sit on the front steps at night, bare feet, sharing a bottle of beer?

How could you believe him, a boy like the ones who wait in the alley for me, a clean shirt and a twenty-dollar bill in their pocket? An arm around my shoulders if I'm lucky?

Tell me these things. Tell me the things I need to know.

———

"Open another bottle of wine, Don," Connie said. She pushed her plate away and stretched her legs onto the empty chair. "We're going to get Martha drunk and keep her here tonight."

"Wrong," I said. "I have to get home soon."

"Hot date?" Don uncorked the bottle and poured. "Anything we should know about?"

"She's going to go home and call Edward. So he can pack her boxes," Connie said, and her laughter was brittle. "So they can lock themselves in the bedroom and do whatever it is they do when she tells us they're busy."

"You sure you need more wine?" Don said.

"Fuck you. I'm fine. I'm not the one sneaking around like some teenager. I'm not hiding out and avoiding phone calls and behaving like—"

"Hey, hey," Don said. He looked at me and I said nothing. "What's this? We're just talking, right? We're just about ready to whip out the after-dinner mints." He reached across the table and took Connie's hand.

"I'm tired of this," she said to me. "I'm tired of the fact that you seem to have no goddamn idea of what's important." She pulled her hand from Don's. "He's making a fool of you. And it may not bother you but it sure as hell bothers me."

I looked around the room. Their first house, in the county. For the schools, Connie had said. It was a good school district. They lived in a new development, eight models of houses repeating irregularly along the roads. There were never two of the same next to one another, or directly across the street. Tar driveways and fresh-laid lawns, seams showing.

She'd wanted a baby for as long as I could remember, a low burn of desperation that came off of her in waves. At her wedding she'd said to me *Now we just have to figure out the best time to have a baby. We have to get out of the city first, but after that . . . when you have one they can play together, Marth. Won't that be great?*

"He's not making a fool of me." *You're all ready*, I thought. *Why are you so angry?*

"Then you're making a fool of yourself." She got up and began carrying dishes to the kitchen.

"I have to go," I said. "Thank you for dinner. The house is beautiful." I turned to Don and hugged him. "I still owe you guys a housewarming gift."

"I'm sorry, Martha." He buried his face in my neck and I smelled the cologne he'd worn for as long as I could remember him wearing cologne, the other boys singing *Hey Donny, you smell awful pretty*, shaking their hips at him and batting their eyes. *Yeah, you know you want this*, he'd say, *you just keep dreaming.*

"Not your fault," I said. "Connie? I'm going. Thanks." She was in the kitchen, scraping plates over the sink. *We even have a garbage disposal! Martha, wait till you see!*

"Bye," she said. She didn't turn.

"I'll call you." Don walked me to the door—*This is the vestibule, powder room's on your left*—and squeezed my shoulders. I had my car keys ready—I didn't want to stop and fumble, to hear anything once he'd shut the door behind me.

I drove out of the development, squinting through the dark, reversing the turns I'd made on the way in. I passed the school, set well back from the road with a wide semicircular drive and a parking lot in front. The buildings were low and brick, streamlined; the windows wide and tall and covered with hand-painted posters and garlands of construction paper. There were covered walkways between the buildings and a grassy courtyard in the center. Well behind all this was a playground.

It's so much better than the city district. It's safe and the teachers are better-trained and the facilities!—my God, it's nothing like what we had.

I backed out of a dead-end street and corrected the turn. Three exits on the beltway and I merged onto the downtown artery, the lights spilling wide and low under a gauzy dark sky. A set of knives, German-made in a heavy wooden block, sharp enough to cut what they're meant to and nothing else. I would wrap and ribbon them. Happy housewarming.

I was happy—I had no reason not to be. There were no dishes to clean in my house, no floors that needed sweeping, nothing to wrap and store in the refrigerator and eat cold from a bowl the next day. My bed was smooth and made, and if there was silence I would swim in it, and if there were voices they would be safe as sharp knives.

There was nothing I wanted that I didn't have.

———

I unlocked the front door and stood in my own vestibule, unlocked the interior door and climbed my steps. The sound of my footsteps was louder now that I'd begun rolling up carpets and boxing pillows, the air dryer, the floor less dusty. I picked up the phone and called Edward.

"You're home now?" he said. A television chattered in the background.

"I'm here. If you want to come over."

"I do. Half an hour?"

"I'll be downstairs."

I hung up and stepped out of my pants, pulled my shirt over my head and brushed my hair. I had no lingerie, nothing red and silky, no white lace, nothing that he would want to play with or watch me take off slowly, slipping straps over my shoulders, fingers running under ruffled edges. I put a robe on and went downstairs to wait.

It was quiet on the street. A couple stood outside the liquor store, talking, fighting, I couldn't be sure. They stood face to face, close enough to touch but her arms were crossed in front of her, his in pockets. He rocked on the balls of his feet. A man carrying what looked like a pile of folded blankets approached them, handed the pile to the woman and walked on. The couple stood then, side by side, silent, for five minutes or ten, until she handed half of the blankets to the man and they separated, walking slowly in opposite directions down the street.

"I tried to call you earlier," Edward said as I opened the door for him.

"I'm sorry." He moved past me, a hand on my shoulder. I locked the door and followed him up the stairs.

"Have you eaten?" he said. I nodded. I went into the kitchen and poured glasses of wine. I brought them out. He was in the bedroom, sitting in the chair by the window.

"Thank you. I want you to take the robe off," he said. He sipped and set his glass on the floor. "Take it off and sit down."

I laid the robe on the bed. I was naked beneath it.

"On the bed is fine," he said. "Sit there. On the edge, like that. Good. Thank you." He reached down for his wine glass and balanced it on the arm of the chair, his fingers circling the stem. He nodded slightly. "Drink your wine. Why don't you put it on the night table? Okay." He leaned forward, his shirt bright white in the dark of the room. "Tell me about your evening. Where did you go?"

"To Connie's. They wanted me to see the new house so they invited me for dinner."

He nodded, smiling. "And how's the house?"

"It's fine," I said. "It's—"

"Martha, please don't lie to me." He drank, pulled a cigarette from his pocket. "Tell me what you thought of the house."

"It's—Edward, I don't know. It's a house. It has two floors and a basement. Two bedrooms. There's—"

"Excuse me for a moment," he said. "There's no ashtray in here."

"In the kitchen," I said, my voice vague, thin. I was suddenly tired. My back was very straight. "On the counter, I think."

"Okay. I'm going to get it. Stay there—you're not uncomfortable?"

I nodded.

"Only a little longer, Martha. I'll be right back." He was gone only for a minute, came back with the ashtray and bottle of wine. He settled into the chair.

"Now. Please—I want you to stop fucking with me. I want you to answer me honestly. You hated the house, didn't you?"

I nodded.

"You thought it was ugly and depressing. You thought the neighborhood was awful. How did you feel?"

"Excuse me?"

"In the house," he said, his voice rising, impatient. "How did you feel while you were there?"

I was very still, silent, and he waited. He would wait for longer than I could sit there. I knew that. "They have a lot of her mother's old furniture," I said. "I remember it from—"

"I'm not interested in the furniture. Straighten up a bit, would you? Perfect. Open your legs just a bit, please. Now slide back some—good. You look beautiful," he said. "There are times when I think you're one of the most beautiful women I've ever known. And diplomatic." He lit the cigarette and laughed softly. "You felt superior. You felt like you were too good to be out there. You think they're pathetic," he said. He shook his head. "Your oldest friends. It amazes me that you can be so smug. And it amazes me that you need me to say all this for you." He stubbed the cigarette out and knelt on the floor in front of me, his hands resting lightly on my hips. "You hated that place and look at where you live, Martha—have you looked out the window recently?" He squeezed my hips, brought his face to my belly and kissed it, looked up into my face.

"That's not true," I said.

"What? That you're smug? That you live in a dump? I'm not interested in what you think is true or not." He stood and walked to the night table, handed me my glass. I drank. "Those people love you, Martha. You should be more generous with them." He picked up the robe and held it open behind me. I put my arms in the sleeves, wrapped and tied it.

"Good girl, Martha," he said. He kissed my forehead, caught my hands and brought them to his shirt, to the buttons. I slipped them open, began to undo his belt. I thought of that house, the furniture I'd known for years in another place and the new pieces, the candy dishes and hinged picture frames and crystal bud vases. I had none of those things. It would not have occurred to me to want them.

I slipped his pants down over his hips. He smoothed my hair back against the nape of my neck and slid his hands around and under my chin, lifting my face up to him. "You should learn to be more honest with yourself," he said, pressing my eyes closed with his thumbs. "And you should learn to be more accepting of other people . . . of their preferences." He moved into the V of my legs. "You're a lucky girl, Martha. When you remember this you'll remember something entirely different than I will."

I imagined him in ten years, in twenty. I imagined his hair, shot through with gray, short enough so that the waves lay neat against his head, his eyes still blue and bright and his hands unmarked by anything more than the most insignificant cuts. My mother had waited for someone for ten years, and then had stopped waiting. We are secrets to one another, I thought, all of us; dark and small in the middle of things, in our houses where our teacups and silver and throw pillows are charms against whatever damage we might do to one another, and how much damage is possible, in ten years or one month? If you balance the accounts, the gifts of perfume and cuff links and candles and crystal against the humiliations and silence and lies, the little indignities that eventually bury you, will there be symmetry, or something close enough to call it that? And if your house is empty, what then?

I woke and he was sitting up, a cigarette burning between his fingers, watching the street below.

"It's quiet," he said. "Are you dreaming?"

"I don't know." He was a shadow in a room of them.

"You're dreaming. You could have anything you wanted." He crushed the cigarette and drew my head into his lap, stroked it. "What do you remember?"

My eyes were closing.

"You live in a beautiful house. Stay here," he said, or I thought he said—I was sinking, there were fallen leaves lapping at my feet, he pulled the blanket up around me and I remember being surprised by this, by the warm silence in the room, almost bare; I remember the couple on the street, carrying the blankets home.

I DROVE FOR TWO DAYS INTO stillness.
I drove west along the narrow arm of Maryland and then south, the
pale sun angling less the farther I went, and warmer, until I was
driving in shirtsleeves, until the road seemed to slope slightly
down, always, as though readying itself to fall away into the Gulf of
Mexico.

I have never lived in a place like this one. My street is flat and
wide, boxy houses set close together on either side with squares
of lawn in front of them and gravel driveways in between. I have
never lived in a house whose walls are its own. When I put my
hand to one of them I do not feel the vibration of a television on
the other side, or the trembling of a headboard.

Everything from my car is stacked in a corner of the living
room. My bed is a sleeping bag opened on the bare floor under a

window, a pillow and sheet on top of it. The phone is plugged into the jack but useless until tomorrow. I lie awake and what I hear is stillness, a solid thing that wraps heavy around me.

The tallest building in town is six stories. Far taller than that are the pines, and they go on for miles, tilting over the road, and the sky at dusk was a sliver of gray disappearing ahead into dark green while I drove straight, shoulders aching, and the trees closed over the road behind me.

The main street is long and straight. Gas stations, tackle shops, diners and thrift stores, a travel agency with a bright yellow beach umbrella on its sign. I made the first turn and the houses were wide and sprawling, with cupolas and etched-glass windows and wraparound porches, and at the end of driveways sheds painted to match the shingles. I made the second turn onto my street and drove almost to the end, to this white house, small and symmetrical in its neat square lot, a door and two windows in the front facade like a child's drawing.

I wait, blinking in the dark. If I sit up and bring myself level with the windowsill I can hear the low brush of pine needles, a breeze high above in the cool dark. There are no human sounds. I get up and wrap the sheet around me, open the front door and step out onto the tiny concrete porch. There are lights in other windows, dim behind blinds and curtains, but the silence is entire.

North, two days north, the neighbors are standing in front of the liquor store on the corner. Girls in hooded sweatshirts balance a toddler on one hip and hold a cigarette in their free hand, nails red and perfectly oval. Men still sit on the front steps—it is not cold enough yet to drive them inside, though it will be soon. The colder it gets the more police cars will stop in front of houses, officers knocking on doors in pairs for what comes over the scanner as a 10–41—a domestic. Women from the seafood packing house crowd around the bus stop bench, laughing, shifting their weight from foot to foot. When the bus stops they stand aside to let a line of women off, and they greet one another, squeezing arms briefly. They will do the same tomorrow. If any of them looked up they could see into my bedroom window, curtains pulled aside and tucked behind nails I left in the wall.

If the girls stand too long, their children will howl and kick at their legs. They pitch their cigarettes into the gutter and hike the babies up on cocked hips—second nature already, and they walk back up the block together, splitting off at corners. They unlock doors and step out of their shoes on small carpets, hand the babies to mothers or boyfriends so they can strip off their clothes and wash their faces. They sleep in rooms that even now are too warm, heavy carpeting snug against walls with rectangles cut from it for the heat registers.

I can see all this, wrapped in my flowered sheet. A light across the street goes off and one in the house next to mine goes on; a faucet runs, then stops, and the window is dark again. Around me the trees go on for days.

———

My neighbor sings to Jesus. I wake in the morning and sit up, shoulders and hips aching, and when I look out the side window I can see across the narrow strip of grass into her kitchen. She stands at the sink, wearing a white cloth hat with a checkered band, her shoulders moving quickly. I can't see her hands, but I can hear her voice, just in tune, just reaching me from across the grass.

O Jesus, I have promised to serve Thee to the end; Be Thou forever near me, my master and my friend.

She turns to speak to someone in the room behind her and disappears from the window. Her husband at the table, I think, newspaper spread out before him, coffee rings on the front page already and a baby in a high chair, sticky bib and slick chin. I imagine her wiping the baby's face with a damp dishrag, pulling toast from under the broiler and pouring juice into a plastic handled cup as she steps over another baby, chewing on a rubber spatula on the floor. I lie back down and close my eyes for what is maybe a minute, maybe an hour, and someone knocks at the door.

"Just a minute!" I shout, and pull my pants on, my shirt; kick the sleeping bag and sheet to a corner of the room. I open the door and she stands there, neat khaki pants and a white sweatshirt, the hat pulled low over her brow. Her face is shadowed under the rolled brim, and she carries a platter covered in aluminum foil.

"I'm Louise. Next door," she says, smiling, and nods to her right. "I saw you come in last night but it was so late I figured you must be tired."

It was not that late, maybe nine o'clock. I think of the silence, and the lights blinking off. "I'm Martha," I say. "Hi. Do you want to come in?" I step back and open the door wider. "My goodness," she says. "Where are all your things?"

She takes in the room, bare except for the suitcase and pile of bags in the corner, the crumpled bedding. "I'm having the furniture delivered. It's supposed to get here tomorrow." A breeze comes in through the open door and I realize I am squinting against the brilliance of the sun. Elongated squares of light illuminate the floorboards, dust motes spiral lazily at our feet. Her white sneakers are pristine, glowing.

"You don't have anything?"

"Electricity," I say, and flip the switch on the wall. The overhead light comes on. The room is no brighter.

"Well, my goodness. Here," she extends the platter toward me. "I didn't figure you had time to go to the grocery store." I lift a corner of the foil. "Biscuits," I say. "Thank you. You really didn't have to do this."

"They're yeast rolls," she says, and smiles still wider. Yeast rolls—I have never heard of such a thing. Her teeth are the color of her shoes. "I was making a mess of them this morning anyway. It's no trouble."

We stand for a moment in front of the open door. *She is my age*, I think, maybe a little older, with the look of someone to whom baking comes naturally. Her eyebrows are pale, nearly invisible, so that above the smile her face is oddly expressionless, a smooth tumbled stone.

"Where is the grocery store, anyway? I didn't see one when I was coming in last night."

"Just up the block and over a few. There's another big street on the other side of the neighborhood, but you probably didn't see it if you came in from the interstate. You could walk it if you wanted to, if you have one of those carts with the wheels—you know those pulley carts? I have one and I love it."

"Great. Thanks. I should probably start stocking the refrigerator."

"Heavens, you don't even have coffee, do you? Why don't you come over to our house? Please," she says, "you can't just sit here in an empty house."

And I agree, without thinking twice about it, something that would never have occurred to me in Baltimore. I saw my neighbors on the street, the ones who worked on their way to the bus stop in the mornings, the ones sitting on the steps when I got home at night. The facades of the houses seemed flimsy for all their brick and Formstone. No one was contained.

"Let me just have a minute to wash my face, okay? And find some clean clothes—"

"You take your time. Is your hot water on? Because if it isn't you could really—"

"No, it's fine. Thank you, though. Do you want to wait? It'll only take a minute."

"Oh no—you just do whatever you need to do and come over when you're finished. Just come in the front door."

She is on the porch before I can say anything else, down the steps and waving as she crosses the wet grass. Her body is a secret, invisible in the clothes she wears—I have no sense of the space she would occupy without them. She waves until she turns to go up her own steps, hands white and vague, the nape of her neck glabrous. I wait to hear her singing but there is only silence.

I close the door behind me and pull clean clothes from the suitcase, soap and a towel and the zippered bag of makeup. The water in the bathroom runs cold. I wash my face, run wet hands through my hair until it is close to soaking. The sun pours in through the window and in the mirror I am haloed, my face a white disk touched by fire.

———

I live here now. I live in a white square house on a street that runs straight and flat and kind—there are no speeding cars to watch for, no chugging buses, no men who stagger and fall, clothes sodden with malt liquor and urine, broken heaps against the curb. I will take walks. I will walk in the early morning and again at dusk, miles in circles, the trees deep green and silent. I will draw the curtains when the sun goes down and not look to see if others have done the same. This is what houses are for—keeping places, floors and walls and roofs fitted around lives, secure. The locks are a gesture, the closed doors are enough. I will understand these things; I live here now. I live in this house, six small rooms, lined neatly against one another in two rows, doorways. I have every intention of learning. I will walk at dusk until the trees eat what daylight's left.

———

Louise's porch has a white wicker loveseat and white wicker planters, a smiling wooden duck wearing an apron and kerchief affixed to the wall by the front door. Her plants are gorgeous, dark green leaves spilling over the edges of the pots, tendrils brushing the wood by my feet. I knock on the front door and open it and the air inside is cool, aggressively so, dark and close and humming with electricity. I hadn't thought I would use the air conditioning till the spring.

"Hello? Louise? I'm here," I call. The front room is carpeted and wallpapered and crowded with furniture: a muted pink sofa and wing chairs, end tables and floral arrangements, lamps with matching patterned shades and a low polished wood table, a crocheted runner along the length of it. One wall is covered by ornately framed photographs set in diagonal rows, staggered down and toward the hallway. Louise and her husband, both blond and fleshy in light-colored sweaters or plaid shirts or vaguely formal-looking clothes, him in a dark jacket and Louise in a shiny red blouse, gold necklace and earrings and long wavy hair. There are no pictures of children.

"Back here, Martha," she calls. "We're in here. Down the hall, kitchen's on the left."

There are more pictures in the hallway but it's too dim to see them. The sun in the kitchen catches me off guard. Louise is pulling mugs from a cabinet. The table is set, place mats and folded napkins. A woman is sitting with a china cup of coffee already in front of her.

"Martha, I'd like you to meet Mrs. Walters. Nana, this is Martha. She just moved in next door."

She's old, this Mrs. Walters, in a bright yellow housecoat, her hair gray and twisted up in silvery pins, hands knotted around the cup in front of her. Nana? Louise's grandmother?

"It's nice to meet you," I say. She nods and smiles, her eyes wettish circles behind thick glasses. "Louise, can I help you with anything? I hate to put you out."

"Not a thing. Just sit down and here's some coffee and we have rolls and jam and bacon and I can make some waffles if you want them—"

"Please, no. This is fine, really. It's more than enough. I don't want to keep you from doing anything you need to do."

There's a sugar bowl in the center of the table, salt and pepper shakers and a duck-shaped syrup decanter. Louise brings platters of food and sets them down. The clock reads nine-thirty.

"Where did you come from, Martha?" the old woman asks. Her voice is neither loud nor tremulous.

"Baltimore," I say. "I'm working down here now. There's a store opening in town, a little jewelry store I'm running."

"Baltimore!" Louise says. She sits and begins loading our plates. "Isn't that a far way? New England, isn't it?"

For a minute I'm not sure what to say. "Not exactly. Not quite. Right by Washington DC. It's below the Mason-Dixon Line," I offer, and the old woman regards me.

"That's right. Nana, didn't you have family in Washington?"

"I had a cousin who married a man from up there. Moved with him," she says, and drizzles syrup from the duck over her bacon. "Lived there almost thirty years." She begins to eat. She balances the fork gracefully, her fingers bent and misshapen but quick.

"Do you live here, too?" I ask.

"She does," Louise says. Her smile hasn't faltered since we've been sitting.

"I lived here with my son," the woman says. "Louise moved in after they got married."

Her mother-in-law. Their house is no bigger than mine—not one of the houses on this street is any bigger than another.

"I saw the pictures in the living room," I say to Louise. "They're beautiful. What's your husband's name?"

"Toby," the old woman says. Her plate is almost empty and Louise forks more bacon onto it, another roll. "My goodness, I forgot the grits," she says, and jumps up to pull a covered pot from the stove.

"What does he do?" I ask. Nana reaches for the duck.

"He's passed on," Louise says. She sets the grits on a pot holder on the table. She reaches for my plate—I've barely touched it—and spoons a steaming mound onto it, white like her cheeks beneath the canvas hat, her smile a pouring river. "When's your husband coming down?" she says.

"Louise, I'm sorry." I have nothing to do but reach for the plate she's holding out to me like a salver, heavy and hot, the grits sliding slowly toward the bacon. There's hardly an inch of table visible under the dishes and cups and platters and my stomach is roiling, nothing but coffee and pretzels and peanut butter crackers for the past two days, empty plastic bags and wrappers still in the foot wells of my car, stained paper cups on the seats. A gray mist falling from the southern Virginia sky, maps and gas receipts, my sweater balled on the seat behind me.

"Your husband?" Nana says. She sops the last of her syrup up with a piece of roll.

"I'm not married," I tell her, and she smiles slightly, pulls a brown pack of cigarettes from the pocket of her dress. "I'm so sorry about your son."

"Oh," Louise says, and spreads her arms. Every surface in this kitchen is covered—toaster, blender, appliances on the counter with quilted cozies over them, a wooden cutting board sticky with dough, an accordion rack filled with brush-painted teacups—"There are so many nice men in this town! Isn't that right, Nana? You let me take you out some night and I'll introduce you around."

I cannot picture her out of this room, and I cannot imagine where she would take me. She reaches up as though to tuck a strand of hair behind her ear but instead pulls at the brim of the hat, tugging it more securely down. There are no strands of hair that I can see, no wisps to come untucked from underneath. Her face is a shadowed moon.

The old woman picks a cigarette from the pack and lights it in one quick motion. She slides the pack across the table toward me.

"Car accident," she says, and sucks on the cigarette, lines knifing around her mouth. "Take one. Drove off the bridge south of town." She might be reading a newspaper article; her voice is even and low. "Two other boys in the car with him. She was here with me." She nods toward Louise, who is scraping plates onto the empty bacon dish and humming under her breath. "Twenty-one years old." She taps her ash into the empty cup. Bone china, translucent.

"Would you like a piece of cake?" Louise says to me. "It's real good, not too sweet." She's made a space on the table for a Tupperware cake container, a plastic dome set into a plastic base. I stand, fold my napkin and lay it on the chair.

"No, thank you. Really. This has been wonderful, but I should—I have to start cleaning." My fingers feel stiff, swollen. I smile at both of them. Nana is complacent, haloed with smoke. "Thank you," I say. "For all of this. It was wonderful." Louise spreads her arms again and for a moment I think she wants to hug me.

"I'm just happy you're here. I don't like an empty house so close by."

The old woman stubs her cigarette out in the cup. She reaches for the pack of cigarettes I haven't touched. "Do you smoke, Martha?" she says.

"Sometimes. I mean I quit for a while and then—"

"I get a special deal on cartons up at the Triangle Mart. Don't buy any before you talk to me."

"Thank you. I won't." My voice hums in my ears.

"If you go past your place to the end of the block and make a right and then your first big left you'll run right into the supermarket parking lot," Louise says. "And if you need anything you come right back over here. Doesn't matter what time, all right? We'll be here."

Yes. Yes. There's a bridge south of town. I'll turn the air conditioner on. The only thing in my house that doesn't belong to me is a plate of biscuits—yeast rolls—on the bare kitchen counter. My house. My house. I'll put the bed in the other front room, in the corner, one window facing the porch, the other the street, and watch.

I OPEN THE STORE AT TEN, five days a week. Sundays and Mondays I do other things. I have to concentrate to name them. Five days of the week I understand and the other two are mysteries, hours stretching wide and deep.

I wear the keys to the jewelry cases on an elastic loop around my wrist. I wear neat black skirts and fitted jackets, high heels. I wear makeup. I wear my hair tucked behind my ears and in my ears I wear earrings picked from the back stock, ornate whorls of silver and rhodochrosite or delicate smoky quartz drops. I wear my nails short and painted dark red and on my fingers I wear wide bands of silver braid. I wear a perfect smile. I wear a watch that tells me when the hours pass. To know that days pass I have to rely on something else.

In the mornings I go through the small stack of applications for part-time help and am interrupted only occasionally by the opening of the door, a woman stopping in to look around. I come out from behind the small cash wrap in the corner and say hello, but I don't hover. I don't follow her from case to case or offer bits of useless information about the jewelry she's looking at. When she leaves I smile, bright, generous, and tell her to come again, and make my way to each case she's touched with paper towels and a bottle of Windex, erasing the five minutes of her life she's spent here.

Other than Louise, who waters her plants in the mornings when I leave, I talk only to people whose names I don't know.

————

When he comes in I'm sitting on a high stool, my fingers black with the sticky residue of tarnish remover, piles of rings sorted by size on the counter.

"Hello," he says immediately. His accent is more northern than mine. "I've been waiting for you to open."

"It's been a few weeks," I say. "But welcome." I wipe my hands on a paper towel.

"I've been out of town." He puts his hands in his pockets and leans over a case. "Nice stuff."

"Thank you." My fingers are gray and waxy. "Excuse me for just a minute. I need to wash my hands and then anything you'd like to see—"

"Take your time."

When I come out of the tiny bathroom in back, rubbing lotion on my damp hands, he is moving slowly from one counter to the next, resting only the tips of his fingers on the edges of the cases. His face is smooth, young, but there are flecks of gray in his hair.

"New in town?" he says, kneeling to peer at a low shelf of cuff links.

"I've been here for about a month. Quiet," I say, and he looks up, smiling.

"Quiet. Yes. Very diplomatic." He straightens.

"Would you like to take a look at those?"

"Actually, some of these in here." He gestures at a vertical revolving case of earrings and I pick up the ring of keys and unlock it for him, swing the door wide and step back. He peers at the tiny rectangular cards pierced with chips of stone. "Left my glasses in the car," he says, and picks up a pair of heart-shaped turquoise posts, the kind of thing you'd buy for your niece. "These'll work."

I lock the case and take the earrings back to the counter, put them in a small box. Fifteen dollars. He pays with cash.

"Thank you," he says, putting the box in his jacket pocket. "And good luck. I'm sure you'll do well here."

For a minute I think he might shake my hand. But he doesn't. He nods and smiles as though he's wrapped up a deal—which I suppose he has—and ducks out, crosses the street and gets into a small car a few yards down. I hesitate before picking up the bottle of Windex. He's left no marks anywhere, the glass shines. And I read through another three applications before I pick up my coffee and look out the window again and see that his car has not moved, that he's sitting behind the wheel, staring straight ahead of him while the traffic light blinks through its cycles.

———

I interview the names on the applications and hire three girls, two still in high school, to work afternoons and Saturdays and one who doesn't look old enough to have graduated but who is somehow available during the day. I check her references and don't ask any questions. I can extend store hours. He comes in again, and again, once every three or four days, faded jeans,

ironed shirt and tweed jacket, smelling vaguely of aftershave. He
buys another pair of earrings, inexpensive and forgettable, and a
herringbone bracelet. I train the girls. I watch, when he leaves,
to see him walk to his car. He drives away immediately. The girls
from the high school are sweet, bright; they stow their books in
the back room when they arrive at three-thirty and drape them-
selves with necklaces, clip mother-of-pearl barrettes into their
hair. They do homework only when there are no customers.
They lay what they've worn in a neat pile by the register before
closing. I trust them.

I rearrange the displays and organize the inventory, I begin re-
pair work on the pieces broken during shipping. He comes in,
two mornings a week, Tuesdays and Fridays. His name is Wes-
ley—Wes. My fingers are steady with pliers and tweezers,
pieces of loose wire and bent prongs. He brings me coffee, he
buys another bracelet, a cheap Mexican bangle. His shirts are
starched. He sits in his car for twenty full minutes one day.

I think of my parents. I think of low blue light in a dark room
and rose bushes pruned back for the winter. I think of Carly and I
tell myself that I will call her, tonight or tomorrow or the next; I
imagine the heavy beige phone in her dorm room and dry heat
piping up from the floor below. I think of her books, highlighted
and stained. I leave the store at six and think that the air is too
warm for it to be so dark, so early. I wave to the girl I've left be-
hind the counter and drive the street, already quiet, make the
two turns and pull up to my house. Louise does not sing at night.
I wash my face and sit in the living room with a glass of wine that
becomes two and then four and the quiet outside is enormous
and the quiet inside is bigger still until it shrinks in upon itself like
curling leaves that come to rest on my closing eyes. I am begin-
ning to want, these nights, or something close enough to it.

Wes is a guidance counselor at the high school. He tells me this one Tuesday over coffee he's brought from the diner down the block. He knows the girls who work for me.

"Melissa and Kerry," he says to me. "Nice girls. How are they working out?"

"They're fine," I tell him. "Have you been cutting classes?" When he comes, he comes between ten and noon. My slowest hours.

"We have two counselors. They stagger us—she's on campus in the mornings and my appointments are after classes end so . . . "

I wonder if he talks to the students the same way he talks to me—the questions that aren't quite questions, the distant friendliness—it occurs to me that perhaps these are ways of drawing them out, of letting them tell him the things he needs to know. *In their own time,* I think. There is a bubble between us; his words float around it.

"So what do you counsel them about?"

"This coffee isn't very good," he says. He tips the paper cup slightly, sloshes the liquid inside. "Mostly academics. If their grades start to drop I talk to them. College admissions. Things like that. Roberta—she's the other counselor—she does the other stuff. Family problems, drugs."

He doesn't quite look at me when he speaks—his entire demeanor, in fact, is made up of almosts, of half-ways—the questions, glances, his steps through the door neither quiet nor heavy, his face of indeterminate age. He could be twenty-five or forty. I could pass my hand right through him. I imagine him behind a desk in a cluttered office, his jacket off, tilted back in a wheeled chair, waiting, while the girl or boy across from him sits miserably, head down, books in a pile on the floor, athletic shoes scuffing beside them.

"So." He checks his watch, fishes in his pocket for car keys. "That's what I do. And this is what you do." And for a moment I think *No, this is not what I do. This is how my days pass. This is my calendar. I used to do other things. But I can't remember now.*

"Do you have a daughter?" I ask him, and for the first time since he's been coming in he seems flustered, just perceptibly, his shoulders and chin rising slightly.

"No. Why would you ask that?"

"What you buy," I say. "Those little earrings. I stock those because that's what people usually buy their kids."

"Is that so," he says, almost smug, as though he's fooled me, caught me in a moment of profound stupidity, and I think of the students. Those poor kids. "They're for my wife. I buy them for my wife."

"Maybe next time you'll let me show you something a little more sophisticated, then," I tell him. I don't hesitate. I smile, and he regards me with something close to loathing. When he leaves he disappears around the block. His car is parked where I can't see, and I stand at the front door waiting for him to drive past, not caring that he might see me there. And I think that there won't be a next time, that he won't come in again because I refused to give him the response he wanted, whatever it might have been.

They're for my wife.

And your wife, why haven't you brought her? Does she know where you bought them? Does she love them? I'd like to meet her or *I'm so sorry to hear you're married* or simply raised eyebrows, a low exhale of breath, something to let him see that he's damaged me.

His car never passes. I wait at the door until it opens and two older women come in, nodding pleasantly at me. Hat pins, they're looking for. I imagine him sitting in the cramped front seat. The car is small, I've seen that much. But perhaps he's just taken a different way home.

———

Louise is at her mailbox when I get home. She waves and calls hello—usually we speak only briefly before I pull my own door shut and lock it, but tonight I have something different in mind.

"Louise," I say. "I was wondering—would you like to come over for a while after dinner?"

"Oh, how nice—but we've just eaten. Nana likes to eat early so I just—"

"That's okay. Maybe in an hour or so then? Around seven? You haven't really seen the house since I got everything all put together."

She's shuffling envelopes distractedly. Every time I've seen her, her hands are moving, busy, never still. She seems unsure of what to say.

"That's sweet, Martha, but I don't—I try not to leave Nana alone for too long." Her hands work, the envelopes small flags in the dark.

"Just for a drink or two. And there's the phone if she needs you for anything, you'd be back in less than a minute. If you want to," I say. "If not, it's fine. We could do it some other time."

"No," she says. She fans the stack of mail into a neat rectangle, bends it U-shaped. "I would like that very much. Thank you."

Her car, an old green sedan, backs down the driveway on Wednesday nights and Sunday mornings, Nana in the passenger seat with a metal walker stowed in the back. And I see Louise on Mondays, walking up the street with the empty grocery cart rolling behind her, a heavy purse over her shoulder and her hat pulled low, and then less than an hour later back again with blue plastic bags bulging out between the bars of the cart. I've never run into her in the grocery store.

She deposits the mail in the box and raises the flag. "Seven?" she says.

"Perfect. I'll leave the door unlocked."

———

Inside, I light candles. I collect the newspapers and magazines and pile them in a corner. I wipe the kitchen counters down and get out glasses and a good bottle of wine, arrange crackers on a plate, a hunk of Gorgonzola, olives in a bowl. I powder my face, reapply eyeliner and lipstick. I bring the food and wine into the living room and brush lint from my pants—for Louise, I think. She's an angel, a visitation. My heart is hammering; my house looks as though someone lives there. The living room is warm, lit yellow from the candles. I switch on a lamp in the corner. It's seduction, somehow.

She knocks on the door at seven exactly and when I open it I see that she's changed her clothes, from khaki pants to a long denim skirt and blue sweater. The hat is a different one, I think, more structured, a dark blue ribbon woven at the brim.

"Oh, Martha, this is lovely! I didn't think you'd go to all this trouble—it's—thank you. It's lovely, really."

"It wasn't any trouble," I tell her. "I'm so happy you're here." And it's true, and a bitter surprise—it's all I can do to keep from drawing her into my arms. Her body is fleshy, I can see that now, and soft enough so that I imagine my fingers would sink down into her. "Sit down," I say. "Can I pour you a glass of wine?"

"Thank you." She nods, smoothes her hands over her lap. I pour and hand her the glass and when I hold mine up she hesitates for a moment before raising her own. I touch the bowl of my glass to hers gently and with the clink she begins to laugh, more musical than her singing.

"I just can't believe I'm here," she says. "I don't really see my old girlfriends much anymore because I'm home with Nana most of the time. And sometimes I think about maybe calling them but they've got kids, most of them, and they're so busy . . ." She drinks and her brow furrows. "This is good wine," she says, and leans into the couch, fingers rubbing semicircles along the base of her glass.

We talk—she talks, mostly. I am cautious of asking too many questions but the words pour out of her like blood from a wound, her smile never faltering, her hands never still: she married her husband after graduating high school and settled into his mother's house, she loved it, this street, that house, still does; they were together there for two years before he was killed in a car accident, he and his friends driving back into town from the river, from fishing, they'd been drinking all day, she knew that, it's what they always did, but it was the other car that jumped the median and hit them head on and so what was the point in blaming him, in wishing he'd done something differently when he'd only done what he always did, every Saturday, the river, the fish?

I'm pouring the wine quickly and she drinks it down without pausing, one hand holding the glass and the other tucked safely beneath her legs. He was a good husband, a good son; the only regret she has, really, is that there were no children—not for lack of trying, of praying, but there's no one to blame for that either and she has Nana now, she has a lot more than some, she thanks God for all of it.

Her face is like milk. I get up to open another bottle of wine and my legs are unsteady; the heel of my shoe catches on the rug and I almost stumble. I haven't eaten since the morning. "I'm listening," I call from the kitchen, and her voice pours on.

The lights next door don't flicker. I bring a new bottle back to the living room. The smell of Louise is filling it, sweet and mild and somehow raw. Or perhaps it's only the candles.

"You're so pretty," she says, her eyes sleepy. "Nana kept saying right after she met you how pretty you are and how I should . . . I should maybe try to do something with myself."

I sit down next to her. Our shoulders are inches apart and I can see that at the back of her neck, around her ears, there are only the downiest tufts of hair, a half-inch if that, almost translucent. She sees me looking and I lean quickly to pour.

"It's all right," she says, reaches for the hat and tugs at the brim, pulling it left then right before centering it again and folding her hands in her lap, thumbs working. "It's the strangest thing." She speaks slowly now and I can hear the wine in her voice, elided syllables and soft consonants. "When Toby died there were so many things to take care of, the funeral and the insurance settlement, so much paperwork, and Nana, and I—I stopped working then because there was so much—and I'd always twirled my hair, you know? Because it was long and most of the time I didn't even know I was doing it, and Toby used to laugh at me because I was always playing with it . . . and after he died I kept thinking that maybe I should just cut it off, it took so much time to take care of, but I . . ." She is still enough so that I can see the rise of her chest when she breathes, the blue sweater, a fine gold chain disappearing beneath the neck of it. "I didn't even realize I was doing it, but I was doing it in my sleep, even, I'd wake up and find all this hair on the pillow—I thought it was just that I was doing so much, you know—don't they say that stress can make your hair fall out? I read that somewhere once. And I thought that was it but it was me, I kept twisting it up in my fingers all the time and I guess I didn't realize how hard I was pulling—can you imagine such a thing?" she says.

She reaches for her glass and cradles it in both hands, laughs and sets it down again. "So I went and had it cut shorter because I thought if there wasn't so much of it . . . I've even tried smoking. Nana used to give me cigarettes and I tried but that didn't work, I hated it, I wish she wouldn't smoke but it's her house, so . . . and I couldn't stop. The settlement was big enough and I was home all the time—the minute I sat down or started thinking about something I'd be pulling at it. Nana has all these wigs." She laughs again and turns to face me. "All different kinds, in a closet at home. I can't stand them—they're all hot and itchy and every time I looked in a mirror I'd jump, almost, because it was like I was someone else. It all looks so nice," she says, and picks up one of the napkins I laid out. "I haven't even eaten any cheese and crackers." She rests the empty napkin in her lap and begins to fold it, pinching the corners smooth. "I don't think I like olives very much. We used to have them on the table all the time, with dinner—in a little dish with celery? Like that? But these look different." She leans and draws the bowl closer, tilts it to her. "Why are they wrinkled?"

"They're cured," I tell her, and she regards me. *Cured*—bed rest, plastic orange bottles of pills, Dixie cups of lukewarm water. Wet washcloths, sponge baths. I imagine her in her bed, long nightgown tangled around her legs, hands working, tearing bits of dreams away, and Nana one room over, smoking by the window.

"Cured," she says. "It's too bad you didn't move here sooner. Toby was always telling me how he thought I should go out with my friends more. He would've liked you. He would've—well." She scoops the bits of napkin up—tattered now, damp confetti—and wraps them neatly in a new one. "I should be getting back. Thank you so much for this. Maybe you could come for dinner one night? I'm sorry I haven't been up to see the store— sometimes I wonder where the time gets to . . . "

We stand and the impulse to hug her is gone—I'm exhausted, it's barely nine o'clock and I have the sense of a long night ahead of me, as though there's still driving to do, an eternity of it; as though I haven't got to the place I'm going yet. But there is nowhere other than here.

———

I watch for the lights to go out. I sit on the couch, picking olives from the bowl, dropping the pits into the empty wine bottle. There's half a bottle left. I'm making my way through it.

He would not have liked me. He would have known with one look to stay away and if you had asked him why he would not have been able to tell you.

He must have loved her hair, the heaviness of it on his chest at night, another blanket, alive.

Were you quiet? Did you worry his mother would hear you, those thin walls? Did you listen for her steps, to the bathroom or kitchen, and cover his mouth with your hand, laughing?

Her husband and her son. She must still be able to see them, in their places at the table, while Louise sings, kneading dough, washing dishes; hands fevered and hungry—what kind of comfort is this?

Ask and ye shall receive.

Her bed must be narrow, and Louise's wide, a picture of Jesus on the wall above it, His eyes turned upward, hair a parted curtain. I run my hands through my own, neatly cut before I left. It touches my shoulders, dark and thick and straight. My father's hair. And Carly has my mother's, finer and lighter, going almost blond in the summer. Two matched sets, one child for each of them, grown and gone.

I wish we'd had a baby. But I have Nana now.

I imagine her tucking the old woman in, kneeling by her bed to pray. No rosaries there, no crucifixes, just Jesus in His robes hanging on the wall.

He walks with me and He talks with me.

But can He cure you, can He still your hands in sleep?

At Mass, my father held me in his lap, carried me with him up the aisle for Communion even before I was old enough for it myself. At night he carried me up the stairs to bed, slid me beneath the covers and tucked them in—*tighter, Daddy, please*—until I could barely roll over, my arms fast to my sides. I felt less comfortable than I did safe, but this was the important thing— safety over comfort, especially in the dark, and when do we forget this and go fearless into bed, kick the sheets down and spread our arms wide for whatever might come to find us there? No child would be so foolish. But my father carried me up, and no man has done this since.

Their house is still dark.

Does sleep come easy for you, does it stay through the night? Or do you dream of fishing and wake, reaching across the bed for what isn't there? Old habits.

I take myself to bed, draw the blankets up smooth over bare skin. All of us, now, are tucked away, motionless or close enough to it. I am still, my face turned toward the window, careful not to move, to offer an invitation to something dangerous. I have been kept from any real harm so far.

THE MAY THAT CARLY GRADUATED from high school it rained every day but two. In the city we secured the screens in windows and set potted plants in sills to catch what fell, left air conditioners off for longer than I could remember in years—sticky heat begins early in Baltimore, but that May was gray and cool and strange. Back yard grass grew long and turned overnight into slick muddy flats. The air smelled not of the harbor but of soil and wet asphalt—the rain had buried the smells of brine and boats under the sopping ground. The air was freshwater, floating down.

I was twenty-three years old and spending my nights with a boy named Nick. He'd moved to Baltimore from DC when he finished school and rented a place not far from the apartment I shared with Connie in a broken-down neighborhood in the north of the city. It was the first time Nick and I had been in the same place for more than a few days—for three years we'd taken trains, borrowed cars, spent weekends in the houses of people we barely knew, crushed the short hours between our skins, wrung them dry until we were dripping ourselves with what was left. We didn't waste time on what was unnecessary. We spoke incessantly, words rushing over themselves in a panic of the ticking clock, a flood; we woke in the middle of the night already speaking, blind and sticky. We buried the words beneath our skins. We slept and didn't dream. Three years of this until I left my parents' house and he came to Baltimore and the clocks stopped, hours endless, overwhelming.

I thought that I would marry him—what else could I think? I had finished everything I knew to do up till then. *I'm here*, he said to me, standing at my door, his loaded car in the lot below, his hair damp and tangled and smelling of something tired, and yes, I thought, this comes next, all this, come in and we'll be quiet because we can, and it will be absolute. We'll sleep through the night.

So we slept, and I dreamt of the man I'd been with the week before: I was sitting at the bar and he came up behind me, a hand on my shoulder, and I turned. He was massive, cracked leather jacket and soft blond hair, a face as wide as the sun. *You're Martha*, he said, *I met you at that party at Winston's.* I remembered—when the bar had closed the week before we'd poured out of it, stumbled the blocks to a house not far, doors open, filled with people I barely knew. I floated from room to room, up stairs and landings until I was on the roof and the only thing over me was milky dark sky. People came and went, moving under it.

Michael, he said. His smile was a long bright day. *Do you remember?*

His apartment was small, the ceilings low. He took up all of it. But on me he was light, so light, the tips of his fingers on my back like something already forgotten even as they lifted me up to him, into the space he filled. *One week*, I remember thinking, and we turned and I was lying on top of him, his body a plateau, wide and forgiving, his hair soft as a child's.

When I woke the next morning he was still, his sleeping skin bright in the dim of the room. I was made of glass.

I got out of bed and collected my clothes from the floor. He sighed and turned, more graceful than a man of his size had a right to be. I stepped into my underwear.

Martha, he said. His face was against the pillow, eyes half-closed, mouth a sweet curve. *Already?*

I sat on the bed and buttoned my shirt. *I have to get ready*, I said. *There's not much time.*

He reached for my shoulder and drew me down, spread his hand across my cheek, his fingers reaching from hairline to neck, easily, the leaf of a tree. *Is this all?*

He was the last of them. For three years I'd done the best I could, which was nothing close to perfect, but enough. When I'd called Nick at midnight, three in the morning, and the phone had rung fifteen times for every minute that flipped green on the clock, I hadn't asked him where he'd been. And he'd returned the favor. Burn the scorecards and bury the ashes, wash the clothes, the hair, the sheets—no need for exorcism, for confession, for penance. Suck the words back in and draw the hands up clean. I had six nights to fade white.

Is this all? Michael's hands were cool and dry and he ran them over me until I was erased, my clothes a shroud covering nothing. His hair spread over my face. I could smell myself in it.

But I didn't dream of this. I dreamt that I was buried in sand, fine and soft, blowing over me like sugar. I raised my arm against the hot weight of it, a surfacing desert snake, and I saw that my skin was eroding, becoming smooth and translucent, and my flesh, dissolving into gold dust and whirling away from me until the arm was a whittled stick of bone. When I woke Nick was unmoving, his forehead damp and creased, miles etched into it, years.

————

Carly was going away to college, something that I hadn't done. I'd driven to classes with Connie and come home in the afternoons, my parents' house as inevitable as breathing. I neither loved it nor hated it—that house, the alleys and corner lots around it, the bars and gas stations and VFW hall—they were the sum total of my life, laid out in a neat grid, navigable. I received my diploma in the mail and packed it along with my clothes and albums to take to the apartment Connie and I had found. For her, it was a stop on the way to someplace else—she and Don had been talking about getting married for years, the church and flowers and rented tuxedo a foregone conclusion, to be put off only until Don found a job that he would be willing to keep for five or fifty years. For me, that apartment was a deep ocean.

But my sister was already packing that May, labeling boxes with fat markers and stacking them along the walls of our old room. She'd been assigned a dorm and a roommate, she was leaving for Delaware in August. In the meantime she was away from our parents' house as often as she could manage.

"So what, are you two living together?" she said. We were sitting in my living room, television on but muted, radio playing. She was working her way through the beer in the refrigerator; I was waiting for Nick to get back from the liquor store. "You have to keep me posted here, Marth. I get no information from Mom and Dad."

"He has his own place. That's all the information there is."

"Right, but he's here all the time, isn't he? I mean he didn't move here so he could take you out on dates." She finished her beer and got up for another. She was wearing shapeless cotton pants and a T-shirt.

"Didn't you say you were going to a party tonight? Where are your clothes?"

"On me. Jesus Christ. Cecilia's having people over but I haven't decided yet. I already know what's going to happen, right?" She let the refrigerator door close and sprawled on the couch, wrapped her shirt around her hand to twist off the bottle cap. "Everyone'll get drunk and loud and try to fuck someone they haven't fucked already. Which will be difficult at this point."

"You're wearing that?"

"Is there a problem?"

Carly was pretty, the kind of pretty that demands nothing: light brown hair streaking blond in summer, wide smile, clear eyes. I'd never seen her putting on makeup or standing in front of her closet, pulling dress after dress off of hangers in search of something perfect. She was nothing like me.

"I'm just wondering if you were planning on wearing that to go out."

"I haven't decided if I'm going yet. God, Martha, you're worse than Mom." She picked up the remote and aimed it at the TV. Pictures strobed: a newscaster at a desk, a woman jumping up and down and clapping on a green carpeted stage, puppies in a basket. Carly tossed the remote to the floor. The puppies' mouths opened and closed noiselessly. "So is he gorgeous? Is he better than anything I've ever seen? Is he cuter than *those?*" She nodded toward the TV. The puppies crawled over one another in a frenzy, tipping the basket.

"You'll see. He'll be here soon."

"So what are you guys doing tonight?" She toed at the remote with a bare foot.

"Probably nothing. This," I said.

"You're not going out? God, Martha, what's wrong with you guys? It's Friday night—take me to some bar where they don't card. Take me someplace where I don't know anyone. Impress me." She stood and walked to the stereo, began spinning the knob up the dial. "I don't understand you," she said. "You used to be out all the time, I remember—I remember you spraying that perfume all over the place and hiking your skirt up once you got out the door"—she settled on a station and sat in front of a speaker, the bottle between her crossed legs. Her hair was smoothed back, held by an elastic. "God, I used to watch you. Those guys—they're all working in gas stations now or something. Seriously. We see them in church." Her voice trailed off and she sipped the beer. She'd never had a boyfriend from what I saw. She'd had dates, boys who came to pick her up for dances or parties and sat in the kitchen to talk to our father while our mother helped her get ready upstairs—she never took the lipstick our mother offered, never let her set her hair in toothed plastic rollers, and they argued—and the boys had held the door for her and walked her out the back yard and down the alley while the three of us stood in the kitchen, washing dishes by the window. Never the same one twice. Later, when I was upstairs with a cup of coffee and my books, I would half-watch from our bedroom window. I would see them, walking slowly to the door—they always walked her to the door—and I would kneel at the side of the window, almost directly above them, their bodies angled as though they were under a Ferris wheel, and wait. They were never there for long: long enough for me to see her rocking slightly in her flat shoes, arms at her sides and then folded across her chest, extra limbs, useless for the moment, and the boy leaning over quickly for a kiss that must have been dry and cold before turning and walking off, long strides, fast, through the chain-link gate that clanged shut behind him. Long enough to see her stand there for another minute, still rocking. I never asked her anything when she came upstairs. But we had watched each other.

"Tomorrow night," I said. "Go to the party tonight and if Mom doesn't want you home tomorrow I'll take you out someplace then. But you're not dressing like that. I'm serious." The metal door to the building slammed and I heard footsteps in the stairwell. I stood. "If you play nice I'll let you borrow something. But I'm not going anywhere with you when you look like you've been sleeping in your clothes."

I expected something—a roll of the eyes, quick words—but she was silent, staring at me from the floor while the deejay babbled on. *For all of you heading down to Chambers tonight they've got two great bands for ten bucks, local boys, so grab your friends and—*

I opened the door as Nick turned the landing corner, wet paper bag in one arm, the shoulders of his shirt soaked through. "It's a bitch out there," he said, and set the bag on the table.

"Nick, this is my sister Carly. Carly, this is Nick." She stood, almost knocking the beer bottle over.

"Carla," she said. "It's nice to meet you. Finally." She walked past him, not looking at me, and went to the refrigerator.

"Did you finish the last one already?" I said.

"So what awful things has Martha told you about me?"

Nick looked at me, eyebrows raised. I shook my head, barely, and listened to the rain, over the radio, a steady drum and rustle from the roof and the leaves of the trees on the hill behind the building, the open sky and dark water, falling constant for weeks until it was a kind of silence in itself.

———

Carly went to the party. She called around until she found some-one who'd be willing to pick her up and bring her back and dis-appeared into my bedroom until the horn honked outside. "Will you still be awake when I get back or do I need a key?"

"We'll be up. Door's unlocked."

Nick poured scotch over ice and we took the glasses to the small balcony, sat on wet plastic chairs. There was another building identical to mine across the parking lot. People were home: televisions flickered, the ringing of phones carried across the damp air. We sat and drank and talked little and were fine, quiet and still. A car pulled into the lot and a man hauled a screaming boy out of the back seat, hoisted him into the crook of an arm and leaned in for a small suitcase and pillow. *Want Mommy, Mommy!* The door to the building opened and a woman stood on the threshold in cutoffs and a T-shirt that glittered faintly. *Hi Barry, hi little man! We've got ice cream upstairs!* The man slammed the car door with his hip and carried the boy up the walkway, handed the suitcase to the woman. She reached up to touch the boy's face and he recoiled, thrashing his head and kicking at his father, words disintegrating into a wail, luminous and pure as silver.

Nick stood and picked up the glasses. "Ice," he said. "You want anything from the kitchen?"

I shook my head and he went inside. I could see inside their apartment: the woman putting the suitcase on a table by the door and the man depositing the pillow and boy onto the couch, the woman turning the television on and going to the freezer, taking out a carton of ice cream and bowls from a cabinet. The boy's father was shaking his head, pacing behind the couch, lips moving. The woman nodded, spooning ice cream into a bowl. The boy himself was invisible, his head below the window ledge. I could see all this.

Nick had been in Baltimore for two weeks, and for two weeks we'd slept every night in my bed. We slept naked, the sides of our bodies barely touching. We didn't wake up to grasp at one another in exhausted desperation, the clock face taunting green; I didn't dial his number in the dark of my room and wait, counting rings, hanging up before the answering machine could click into life. If I woke at night— and I rarely did—I would turn into his shoulder, slide my hands up under the pillow and wait for dreams to fall apart into pieces as safe as torn paper. We didn't have sex. When I got into bed he turned on his side and pulled my arm over him, cupped my hand in his at his chest, stilled it. I slept with my lips to his back. I didn't ask for anything more. He was tired, I thought, from the move and then from his job, the hours; he wanted to be there, else he would have slept at his own house. He is happy, I told myself, and I had no reason to believe otherwise.

"For you," he said. He handed me a fresh drink and kissed my mouth—I remember thinking of it in this way, *my mouth,* as though he were not kissing me but rather a discrete part of me, a small piece that he knew. "What's going on?" He nodded toward the building across the lot.

"Ice cream. The guy looks upset." He was still visible, standing in the kitchen with the woman, their heads close together, lips moving. "I think the kid's on the couch."

"Barry," he said, and laughed. "Barry didn't look too happy either." He sipped from his glass. "Are you cold?"

I shook my head. The air was cool, the rain dissolving into mist, but the scotch had heated my face and hands. My neck was damp with sweat.

He stared across the lot. There were still lights in some windows but no movement. Headlights splashed over the asphalt below and a car pulled up under us. The door opened and Carly stepped out, unsteady, leaned back in to say something that was swallowed in the music coming from the open door. She slammed it behind her and turned, disappeared below us. The door to the building sucked open. I stood.

"Your sister's a pretty girl," Nick said. He reached for my hand. In his, my own felt cold.

"My sister's drunk." I collected the empty glasses and we went inside. The heat of the room was overwhelming; the bottle of scotch sat on the coffee table, half empty. "I need to take care of her."

"What about you?" he said, reaching for my shoulders. "You're swaying."

"I'm fine." I stepped out of his grasp. I'd been fine outside. Now, my hands felt thick and unwieldy as mittens. "Why don't you go to bed? I'll put her in Connie's room."

"Are you sure that's a good idea?"

I could hear her on the steps, slow and deliberate. "Or the couch. Whichever. We'll be fine," I said. I tensed my fingers, spread them. "Go on. I won't be long."

He picked up the bottle and his glass. His shirt was open to the middle, chest narrow and damp and already tanned. I couldn't imagine how he'd got so dark, where he'd been. *Here*, I thought. *He's only been here,* but I stared—how had I not noticed this? His skin was the color of toast.

———

I sat on the bathroom floor, my back against the tub.

"Twice and I was done," I said. Carly knelt in front of the toilet, her shirt off, crumpled in her lap. "Extensive research. If I threw up twice I knew it was safe to go to bed. It might be genetic, if you're lucky."

She shook her head. Her hair was knotted at the nape of her neck, her lips swollen. I'd cleaned the day before and the room smelled faintly of bleach. "I want to stay here. You can go to bed if you want but I think I'll just . . ." She rested her forehead on the lip of the bowl.

"Here," I said. I held out a folded washcloth. "You're going to bruise your head." She took it silently. There was a glass of water and a plastic bottle of Coke on the floor between us. I drank from the Coke. I felt giddy, happy—I'd taken aspirin. The worst for me would be a headache in the morning, if that.

"You came home drunk all the time," she said. "I could hear you falling into things. They never caught you."

"Water." I handed her the glass. "Careful. You should finish this. I always made sure I got sick at other people's houses." But this was not quite the truth—only once or twice had I misjudged my capacity, a long time ago, and then I'd been so careful, so quiet; I'd run the water in our bathroom full force and wiped every surface clean. But after that I'd been vigilant. At other people's houses I was one of the few left standing.

"Of course you did," she said. "You're really good at keeping secrets."

She sat back against the wall and looked at me. Her bra was faded blue cotton, flimsy elastic and soft wrinkled cups. It looked like one I'd had when I was thirteen. It could've been the same.

"Yeah, I know. Stupid. Yours is leather or something, right?" Her cheeks were white, the skin around her mouth red and blotchy. We were angry with one another, sudden as hunger.

"Nothing's stupid," I said. "Drink your water."

"No, let's see." She set the glass down and tossed the shirt from her lap, leaned over and pulled at my collar. "Come on, Martha. Let's see, take your shirt off. Save you time for when you go to bed, right?" Her arms were like tissue and I swatted her away.

"I'm trying to take care of you—maybe you noticed?"

"I'm fine," she said. She sat back heavily on the tile. "You can go. You won't have anything to tell."

"Carly, you're not making sense. How much did you drink, anyway?"

"They wait up for me, you know. Mom does. She—I don't get it. All those assholes, those *Vinnies*—" She spat the word out like something rotten, eyes dull and furious. "You paraded them around like meat on sticks and Mom never said a word to you."

"No, Carly. She—"

"She didn't, Martha. She kept giving you all that fucking perfume and makeup and she'd just go to bed after you left the house like she'd done her duty, like it was some *service* she was providing and it was fine and fucking dandy for you to be running around with them because they went to *church*." She smoothed the shirt out on her lap and pulled it over her head, managed to thread her arms into the sleeves. "So you think my underwear's stupid. Of course you do. It's—she waits in our bedroom for me to come home." She dipped her fingers into the glass of water and rubbed at her face and neck. "I love it." She shook her head and began to laugh. "I fucking love it. You were greasing all those stupid shitheads and she was *married* to one when she was my age and she sits on the bed biting her nails till I get home. You're both liars," she said. She kicked at the rug and lay down on the tile.

"You look like her," I said. Her hair had come loose from the elastic and fanned over the side of her face—before, I'd seen the resemblance that each of us bore to both of our parents, their features echoed crudely in our faces and smudged into something new and the same all at once. It was the first time I'd seen it, my mother's face stripped of years and weather.

"Let me ask you something." Carly closed her eyes. Her lashes were matted and damp. "What are you going to do when you go

to bed tonight? Because I don't know." She propped herself on
one elbow, opened her eyes. Her shirt was hiked up around her
waist and it occurred to me that I couldn't remember the last
time I'd seen her naked. From the time she was ten years old
she'd changed in the bathroom or under her sheets—her skin
was foreign to me, exotic. "I'm telling you the truth. I would've
told Mom but I'm telling you—I don't know. So maybe you
could explain it to me. So I'll know. Because apparently it's im-
portant to the two of you and I don't want to disappoint any-
one." She looked at me, waiting. Her head bobbed slightly; her
left eye was narrowed, focusing.

I had never lied to her, as far as I could remember, and there
was no one thing I hadn't told her—it wasn't that I wanted to
hide things from her. We lived in that house and the people
around us were unchanging, the five years between us inconse-
quential. Anything I could have told her she'd know in time for it
to matter.

"Why are you angry at me?" I said.

"I'm not."

"Carly—"

"I would have to be angry at you every minute of every day for
it to make a difference. People were asking about you tonight,"
she said. "How sad is that? A few of those dirtbags were at the
party. They said they graduated with you." She snorted, sipped at
the water. "I don't remember their names but they looked like
they lived in their Camaros or something. Nick's a big step up,
Martha. He could be pumping gas at the Amoco and he'd still be
a step up."

"Fuck you, Carly," I said. I wasn't angry with her; that had left
me as suddenly as it came. I was afraid, sitting in my small bright
bathroom with my sister, her hair stringy, hands unsteady. I
couldn't remember the last time we'd been alone together for so

long. She was a strange animal, cornered and sick; she would bite.

"You're pathetic," she said. She was smiling. "People like that ask about you and you're not even embarrassed about it. And what, you couldn't get enough? Is that why it took you so long to move out? And this is it—this is the thing—" her smile widened, the breath caught in her throat and her shoulders began to shake and I reached for her, thinking that she would be sick again but it was laughter, miserable barks of it. "They don't want me—can you stand that? It's great—you went through them like Kleenex and you were too fucking *proud* of yourself to even laugh at them with me afterwards and they won't even look at me. Poor Daddy," she said. She was in my lap, shaking, choking with laughter. "You and Mom should've taken it on the road."

I held her. She let me hold her. I smoothed her hair from her face, kept one hand on the glass of water, waiting for her to want it. I waited for her to sleep. *People like that*—their parents had grown up with ours, gone to school together, worked together; their children had done the same. Like that, like us. I helped her into Connie's bed, left the glass of water on the night stand. *Wanting* is for what you can't have. We'd had one another all our lives, those boys and I—birthday parties, school trips, skin and soft lips and stupid eager hearts in the backs of cars, in alleys and basements; we'd licked each other's tears. It didn't matter to me what they had done, were doing—they were my life, the entirety of it.

———

"Is she sleeping?" Nick said. He lay in bed with a magazine.

"Yeah. Is there any scotch?"

He handed me his glass and I took it, sat on the bed. "Bad night. I think she's getting nervous about leaving," I said.

"She should've gotten together with old Barry."

I looked at him.

"Across the street," he said. He smiled. "Ice cream all around."

I set the glass down and slid beneath the covers, rested a hand on his chest. My fingers were ghostly white on it.

"I need to get up early tomorrow, start getting my place together. Still doesn't look like anyone lives there." He kissed my hand, tugged at the blanket and turned into the pillow. I turned the light out.

I lay there, listening, the rain a breath, a slow exhale. I touched my hand to his back, his hip; slid it around to his belly. "Nick," I whispered. I waited; he was too still for sleep. I heard the rain and waited for what came after.

My MOTHER TELLS ME THAT as a baby I was difficult. *You cried, you cried all the time. I didn't know what to do with you—your face got so red! And you would scream, I couldn't believe that a baby could scream for that long. I'd put you in the crib and you'd go on—it scared me. I'd leave you there and when you quieted down I'd go in to check on you and you'd still be crying in your sleep and I'd pick you up to make you stop and you'd start screaming again.*

And after that, nothing, as far as I recall—how is this possible? I cried over bee stings, or being sent to my room for something I'd done wrong, but this is all. When I try to remember something more, some perfect fury, hot and red, there's nothing, and how can I trust this?

Carly wasn't quite as bad, but almost. The strange thing is that you were the only one she'd really calm down for. I would try, and your fa-

ther, and sometimes it would work, but all you had to do was go in and stand by the crib so she could see you—she'd smile and reach for you and that would be it. Every time. Do you remember that? We have a picture somewhere, I think.

I think of our mother, her lovely clothes wrinkled and stained and washed until they were faded, ordinary; her lipstick forgotten, walking the upstairs hall with one or the other of us held close, pitching and screaming as though her arms were made of fire. I imagine our father on the steps, halfway up, one hand on the railing and the other holding a pacifier, a stuffed terrycloth animal. *One of these? Is she hungry? Does she want something?* and our mother walked, voice low and sibilant, no more aware of him than of the sky, no closer than that.

In the photo album from my first Christmas she wears a green velvet dress. In the pictures the dress is dark, darker than the tree behind her, with a collar of white lace. Her cheeks are flushed, deep and even as setting suns. I imagine my father, backing up slowly, camera in front of him, trying to get as much into the frame as possible—the piles of gifts, ribboned and shining, the angel on top of the tree. But what he settles on is his wife, only her, in a moment when I am somewhere else, safely in the playpen, a fat plastic ring in my mouth, quiet for a minute or perhaps not; he trains the camera on his wife, her hair a shiny bob and a glass of wine in her hand, lips parted, smiling, ready to drink. In that moment she was no more a mother than I am now. I imagine my father clicking the shutter and setting the camera down, wading through wrapping paper and boxes to where she stands, waiting for her to drink from the small gold-rimmed goblet before taking it from her and leading her to the couch, his wife in that velvet dress with velvet skin beneath it, her lips stained red, hair streaked gold. I imagine that I was forgotten, left to stare at the blinking lights, safely away from the ribbons and tape while my father drank from my mother's glass and placed his lips on hers, opening them for the wine to run warm into her mouth, to feed her like that.

She is no longer beautiful. In the photo albums there are fewer and fewer pictures of her and more of us, of Carly and me, pretty little girls, quiet and compliant after our first few months in the world, as though we'd got used to something. Turn the pages and our mother's hair goes brown, then grayish; she wears her shirts long and untucked. Camouflage. Carly and I lengthen, our legs, our hair, and our mother moves toward the edge of the frames or behind us, a hand on each shoulder, and it is as though beauty is a fixed quantity, neither created nor destroyed but yielded, a merciless transaction. And in this respect, of the two of us, Carly was the luckier.

I look for evidence. I look for a picture of myself caught un-guarded, not ready, lips downturned and sullen. There is none. In every picture I am smiling, and there is no reason for me now to be so suspicious of this. I was happy, I was safe, I was loved. I was not jealous when Carly was born—by the time she'd been home a week the lines were drawn. She was my mother's but I belonged to my father. One of us for each of them, and it stayed that way until much later, until we were old enough, until it was clear to my father that he lived in a house full of women he didn't know.

What are little girls made of? he used to sing to me, my hands in his, both of our nails bitten short. *Sing, Martha.* I sang, I pulled the St. Christopher's medallion from under his shirt and moved it along its chain, keeping time. Everything nice. Butterflies, birds, seashells. Feathers, hooked beaks, sand, bits of glass.

There was a little girl who had a little curl right in the middle of her forehead. When she was good she was very, very good, and when she was bad, she was horrid.

My hair was straight; I wound it in my mother's rollers.

What are they made of, Martha? Scraped knees, scabs. Pink perfume in plastic bottles, tiny earrings. Our mother had our ears pierced before we could walk, cleaned the gold studs with peroxide. By the time I started high school I'd added more, forcing needles through the lobes. *What else?* Cotton candy, cheap wine, blood. White lies, a few dollars in a pocket, cinnamon drops, ashes. By the time Carly started high school she'd long since taken her earrings out; she wore no jewelry at all. *What else?* Silence. Secrets.

———

Nick said to me *This isn't working. This is not what I want right now*, he said. *I'm sorry. I should've known before.*

Not working. Like a radio, or a VCR. Like medicine, a round of antibiotics and no break in the fever, the infection. He'd been in Baltimore less than a month. He did not say that he didn't love me. This was before I knew that the words were unnecessary to the truth of the thing.

I helped him carry boxes to his car. I believed that if I did this, if I didn't resist or argue, I would be rewarded—a phone call in a month, a letter, paper brittle and translucent, ink smeared. So I carried boxes and stacked them neatly in the trunk and listened to what his plans were, a doll, a fool.

Not working. Everything worked—my arms, legs, my lips and fingers and teeth. My mouth worked, the smooth roof of it, the swallowing throat; it kissed and sucked and bit, it was quiet, it was good, a good girl's quiet mouth, no questions, no *Promise me* no *Please* or *Please don't*—what would they give for a girl like that, for a mouth like that?

I went home and called my mother. *He left*, I told her. She had never met him. *I'm fine*, I said, *don't worry. I just wanted to tell you. So you knew.*

I don't need to know, she said. Then, *Are you all right?*

Fine. I just said. I clenched and unclenched my fingers, let my head fall back and felt the stretch in my neck. I crossed my legs. Working, all of it. I heard water running somewhere in my parents' house.

Your father's out back with the hose. I put some herbs in the other day—all that rain last month and now, nothing. You'll forget, she said. *You'll think of it one day—you'll think it happened to someone else.*

———

Almost ten years later and I remember every particular of that day: the slant of late-June sun, perfect and gold through the leaves of the trees; the faded hopscotch grid chalked on the sidewalk where I sat by his car; the empty beer bottle just behind the front tire. I toed it into the gutter. I remember the shirt I was wearing—a faded gray T-shirt worn handkerchief thin, neck stretched, seams frayed so that the only thing holding it together seemed to be the scent of my perfume. I remember the feel of his body when he held me at the curb, light and wire-strung.

All of this is as close as breath that fogs a mirror. What's gone is my own solid presence; I have no memory of the space I filled. That body is not mine, it wouldn't fit me anymore—reed-thin, too quick to be graceful, easy to carry or release. The skin of it was bright with wanting, pale and ready to be burned clean through to bone. I think of my mother—*You'll think it happened to someone else,* she said, and it's true. I've forgotten what it feels like, that papery skin over something almost weightless. Want is not heavy—it has no history, no story to tell, it invents itself out of small things: a hand on a steering wheel, the frayed collar of a jacket. Present tense and future and nothing else.

When he held me by the car I felt how ready he was for the sun to sink into the road in front of him. Future tense—*I will, I am going to.* I thought the hot pulse of his skin would dissolve that shirt I wore. I lost it, months later, on a gray cold Sunday morning when I pulled my sweater over my head and left someone else's house, caught the bus back to mine. So it wasn't lost, exactly—I'd left it, forgotten it, and I imagined that it would end up in a pile of clothes in the cluttered bedroom and he would pick it up one morning, try to put it on and realize his mistake.

I remember all these things but the body in the middle of them is gone, dissolved like sugar in water. I would recognize it in a picture, concave stomach, thin wrists and a smile, always a smile. I smiled as he drove away, my face breaking open like fruit left too long in the sun. *Aren't you angry?* Carly said to me after our mother had given the phone to her. *That fuck. Why are you so calm?*

She was beautiful by then. She was ready to leave us and she could afford anything. I sat in my empty apartment with the phone warm at my ear and breathed into hers while my father watered the herbs. He was the second husband, although our mother never referred to him as such. Whatever had happened to her before him had happened to someone else.

There's no point, I said to her. *We just—we're trying this out. It's a good thing.*

How can you think that? I don't understand you, Martha. I never have.

I thought of all the boys, the ones who'd promised me forever if I looked at them for longer than a minute and the ones who'd left her in her party dresses at the back door. There was no reason for it—she would have let them do anything if they had tried. I knew that. But they hadn't tried.

You have to give them time, I said. *If you give them time—*

What? They'll come back?

She wanted to believe this as much as I did.

My body then was unfinished, waiting and perfect.

I GO TO LOUISE'S FOR CHRISTMAS.
"Please," she'd said to me, over and again, "We want you to come.
And besides, you can't stay over there by yourself. It wouldn't be
right."

So I wake early on Christmas morning and lie in bed, turn on
my side and stare through the sheer curtains. I pick up the phone
to leave a message at my parents' house. They're at Mass, the
three of them, Carly home for two weeks or one—as little time
as she can manage before packing her car again and driving the
few hours back to school. After Mass they'll walk the few blocks
to my father's sister-in-law's house to drink Anisette and eat
cookies with the cousins and their children. The dining room
will be too warm, sticky from the heat of the oven and the peo-
ple there, children crawling under the table in patent leather

shoes and scratchy creased pants, clip-on ties, hair slicked down
or wound with ribbons. Neighbors will stop in on their way to
their own houses, gifts and plastic shopping bags under their
arms.

I get out of bed and take a blanket to the living room, turn the
television on to the Weather Channel. Twenty-nine degrees,
clear and sunny in Baltimore. There were a few years, I remem-
ber, that it snowed for Christmas; a Christmas Eve when we
stood on the porch and stared up into the silver halo of street-
lights, flakes spinning down on the empty street, and listened to
that odd soft silence like velvet. There was a year when Christ-
mas morning dawned sixty-five degrees and people walked the
blocks like it was Easter.

I doze on the couch, the blanket bunched under my chin.
Louise and Nana are at church—Louise invited me there as well
but I told her I would be going to Mass on my own. I meant it
when I told her that; I'd checked the schedule on the sign in
front of the one Catholic church in town, ironed clothes and
hung them on the closet doorknob. But my eyes won't stay open
long enough to consider the trip to the shower, and the holiday
music that the Weather Channel plays is lulling—snatches of
dreams are almost animated, cartoon figures flitting behind my
eyes so that when I open them the room itself seems like a faded
movie reel.

I sleep for another hour or so before my eyes open for good
and I begin to click the remote at the television, abbreviated
news shows and religious programming, choirs in satin robes
clapping their hands above their heads, swaying like an ocean.
The phone rings. The answering machine picks up—I've turned
the volume all the way down but I can hear the tape running for
almost a minute before it clicks off. I can wear the clothes I laid
out to Louise's. In the refrigerator is a basket I put together,

cheeses and crackers and little jars of marinated vegetables, and a good bottle of wine on the counter. I had thought to bake a cake, or bring something Louise could put on the table with the meal, but there's nothing I know that would be safe. With the basket, I thought, they wouldn't feel obligated to eat anything in front of me; they could push what they didn't like to the back of the pantry.

And I feel a sick wave of self-pity rising in me and then shame, bitter and hot. *This is what I wanted*, I tell myself. *This is what I came for.* I called it solitude I called it necessary I called it right; I packed and drove as though every mile would peel a layer of me away until I arrived stripped clean enough to pass for new. *I've lost nothing*, I think, *nothing of any importance, and I have no right to this.*

I get up and go to the kitchen, pour myself a glass of wine. It's almost eleven. Louise told me to come over at one. Plenty of time. I carry the glass out onto the front porch, arrange the blanket around me on the wooden bench in front of the living room window. I'd imagined winter in the South would be soft and kind and I think of the cold in Baltimore, the sun and blue air like stained glass. But the sky above me is low and gray; the thermometer by the door reads just above forty degrees, neither warm nor cold, the air still and flat like nothing I've ever felt before, weather from some other atmosphere. The quiet on the street is no different from the quiet of any other day.

———

I shower and wash my hair, blow it dry with a round brush and spray it to set the curl. Makeup, red lipstick—my mother used Cherries in the Snow. It smelled of some faint perfume, sophisticated, elegant. The lipstick I wear now is hypo-allergenic, fragrance free, not tested on animals; a simple white cylinder, no faux-tortoise finish or gold band. It feels like wax and tastes like nothing. I wear a narrow skirt and black sweater, tourmaline earrings, translucent green striated with pink. It's twelve-thirty. Louise's car is in her driveway. I hadn't heard them pull up.

I pour my third glass of wine and sit on the couch again, flip channels on the television. The light on the answering machine is flashing and I consider calling back: a perfect excuse not to talk too long. *I only have a few minutes*, I'd say. *Dinner next door— Louise, remember I told you about her? But I wanted to wish you—*

The channels are showing movies, mostly black and white, women in fur collars and muffs and men in narrow pants and topcoats, soap flakes quivering in their hair. When I was younger, there were Christmas parties in the church basement. Connie and I would call one another after dinner, report on our gifts. *Should we go?* she'd say. *Don says he's going over later. We could meet there and then go to Sticky's. His parents always work the soup kitchen Christmas night.*

Sticky. His name was Frank Bucara and summers when we were younger he'd get bomb pops from the Good Humor truck, let them melt down his wrists, a stain of red and blue. One night at a party I'd let him take me into someone's bedroom and we'd lain on the bed, nose to nose. He'd pulled me on top of him and squeezed my legs to his sides, bucked uselessly under me for long minutes. I'd pulled my sweater over my head and bent over him, pushed his shirt up under his chin. His skin was cold and damp. He shoved me from him and ran into the bathroom, knocking over the can of beer he'd carried up with him, and vomited into the toilet. I waited on the bed.

Nice, he'd said when he came out, wiping his chin with his shirttail. *Fucking nice going, Martha. You say a word and I'll make you sorry.* The beer can puddled at his feet.

So why don't we go? Connie would say. *Meet me by the Exxon and we'll see what's going on.*

And I would leave the house early to wait for her, sitting on the curb by the gas station and watching the windows of the row houses, the blinking lights and Nativity scenes like the one in our own window, the doors opening occasionally for people to crowd into vestibules, hugging and stacking boxes into one another's arms before walking slowly down the street and loading into cars, and the silence after they'd driven away was entire, the dark sky like glass and the stars like Frank Bucara's eyes, cold and perfect.

———

"Merry Christmas!" Louise says when she opens the door. She takes the basket and bottle of wine from me and moves aside to let me in. "You look beautiful!" I hadn't bothered with a coat. The house is warm, more so than my own, and I can smell meat roasting.

"And to you," I say. "It smells wonderful in here." Nana is sitting in an armchair by the tree, her hair curled and perfect, her sweater crocheted with poinsettias. "Merry Christmas, Mrs. Walters." The tree is smallish, boughs bent and almost invisible under layers of garland and tinsel. The television flickers with one of the movies I'd flipped past earlier.

"It's good to see you, Martha. Did you do good business this week?"

"I did," I say. "I had a lot of people coming in at night. The girls say it's pretty empty after six but the past few weeks have been crowded, and they were buying." And it was true—I'd been staying late, not getting home until after eight most nights, taking most of the cash from the register with me to deposit first thing the next morning when I'd stop at the bank on my way back to the store, coffee steaming in the plastic cup-holder on the door, smiling at the teller in the drive-thru window. I smiled almost ten hours a day.

"You make sure they buy," Nana says. "People here are cheap. They think they can throw down a five-dollar bill and have their pick of the place."

"Look what Martha brought us," Louise says. She's put the basket on the coffee table and she turns it slowly, pressing her fingers against the cellophane to smooth it over the boxes and jars inside. She unties the ribbon and begins to pull the food out, arranging the packages on the table, making sure all the labels face forward. "Nana, did you see?"

Nana leans forward in her chair. "Louise, why don't you get Martha a drink?"

She brings me a glass of punch, pink and foamy, sherbet and some sweet alcohol that coats my mouth. Nana has her cigarettes and for the first time in years I find myself wanting one, wanting that thin burn in my throat to cut the stickiness. Nana asks me about my family and it occurs to me that she looks old enough to be the grandmother of Louise's husband rather than his mother. She smokes and drinks something that is not punch, it could be iced tea or bourbon but I'm not close enough to her to smell it on her breath. Louise sits on the floor, her corduroy jumper spread out around her, a green turban on her head. It's incongruous, lush and velvety; her face below it is like white cotton beneath an emerald, incidental and pale.

The afternoon passes. Louise refills my punch conscientiously but I'm unable to get drunk; every word I speak is stilted and polite and coated with the sugary stick of the punch. My mouth, my fingers, feel stuffed with gauze, spongy and white, and all at once the heat of the room is suffocating, alive with intent, and the voice in my head is my voice at five years old, on my mother's lap in my mother's ear at a neighbor's house, *I want to go home,* but I haven't spoken aloud. I stand and excuse myself to the bathroom down the hall. The room is small and pale blue and smells faintly of dime-store soaps in a fluted glass bowl near the sink. I run water and splash my face, mascara in black smudges under my eyes, my lipstick worn off, and *home* is a mystery, a thousand miles or twenty feet away, twenty steps across the cold lawn and into the living room, small and square and quiet, unlit candles on the coffee table, a wine glass and a neat stack of magazines, blanket folded over the back of the couch, the ticking of the radiator, everything cool and dark and still.

There's a knock at the door. "Martha," Louise says, "I'm going to take Nana into the kitchen now. Come on in when you're ready."

"I'll be right out." The towels on the rack are tiny, embroidered with gold bells and fringed, and my face and hands are enough to soak one of them, the fibers dark and crushed flat.

"Take your time," she says. "I'm going to open that bottle of wine, if that's all right."

"It's fine, Louise. Of course," I say, but I'm speaking into the weave of the towel and the water's still running and if she's heard she doesn't answer; her steps down the hall are quick and heavy, the steps of a little girl in dress-up shoes who wants to hear the smart click of heels. I re-drape the towel over the rack but leave the water running and open the mirrored cabinet. Air fresheners, dental floss, denture adhesive, a glass jar of cold cream, and on the bottom shelf, aspirin, arthritis ointment, but none of the white-lidded yellow bottles of prescription medications I expected to find, lined up like toy soldiers, ready to save. For a minute I can't imagine such a thing, such a lack, they must be in Nana's bedroom. I hear the oven door squeak open. I swallow four aspirin, turn off the faucet and light as I leave.

———

Louise is twenty-two years old. This is the whole of Christmas dinner for me. There is turkey and stuffing and dishes of vegetables, salty and swimming in butter; the bottle of wine, bourbon and soda on the counter within easy reach over my shoulder; a portable tape deck playing carols, pedal steel and mandolin, tinny and sweet in the room; pies and cookies but what I eat, what I drink, is that Louise is twenty-two years old. She announces this as she serves us, says her mother would never believe that her youngest daughter would be such a good hostess at twenty-two. And there is nothing I can say, there is no way for me to compliment her without giving myself away, so I lower my head and spread the napkin in my lap and reach for the glass of wine before the prayer. I'd imagined her to be in her thirties, and worn for that. I think of Carly, her blond hair and frayed jeans, her roommate and textbooks and plastic cups of flat keg beer; I imagine her late to class on Monday mornings with a donut in her hand, her hair tucked into a baseball cap, sliding into a seat in the back row and leaning over to ask the girl sitting next to her what she did over the weekend. I imagine her asking Louise this.

"Martha, would you like to say grace?" Nana says. She regards me with a slightly arched brow, and it's clear to me that Nana could explain things, could tell me everything Louise would not, not after three glasses of wine or three bottles; would sit across from me and share her cigarettes and explain to me what's happened here, what's happened to her daughter-in-law's body, the sagging body of a woman in the songs I hear on the radio in this town where the trees stop long enough to promise something that I can't find.

Louise sits and folds her hands at the edge of the table. She smiles at me and I imagine that I smile in return. My father says the prayer on Christmas; we do not call it *grace*. Grace is something I don't have.

"Dear Lord," I say, "Thank You for this food, and our houses, and our families. Watch over us in the coming year; keep us close to You. Remember the people who have left us to go to a better place. Grant them peace, and grant us the same." I hesitate. Their heads are bowed, and I wait to see if either one of them will speak, *special intentions* we called them in grade school, the pause in the morning prayer for Connie to ask that her grandmother get better (she did) or for Tim Scallone to ask that we pray for his brother's operation to go well (it did not). Louise and Nana look at me expectantly. I imagine that when I get home I will look in the mirror and see the face of a middle-aged woman. The air here, the framed photos on the wall. "In the name of the Father, the Son, and the Holy Spirit, Amen."

"We're so glad you're here," Louise says. "It's important to be with people during the holidays." She reaches across the table and lays a hand on my wrist and it's all I can do not to swat her like an insect, snatch my arm away to someplace safe, and I have felt more shame today than I can ever remember. I fork turkey into my mouth. How long would it take to eat twenty-two years? Soft flesh, I think, the warm pink air of this house spinning around it like cotton candy, melting in and sweetening everything it touches until it falls off the bone.

I rest the knife and fork on my plate and pour myself more wine.

"Did you talk to your family today, Martha?" Nana says. She eats steadily, neatly as a debutante.

"We'll talk tonight. They're out of the house early on Christmas, visiting people." I think of the light blinking on my answering machine, the clean kitchen counters.

"We used to have an open house here," she says. "When my husband was alive, and Toby was a little thing. Before you knew him." She nods at Louise, who smiles on. "We had people in right from church, from noon till I don't know when. Late." She shakes her head, the corners of her mouth curling up. "When he got older and his friends came over and they were so big, could barely fit all of them in. Snuck drinks in the kitchen, too. Do you have brothers or sisters, Martha?"

"A sister. She's your age," I say to Louise, and I drink, nothing lodged in my throat, no bones, no years.

"My older sisters were awful to me," Louise says pleasantly. She spoons sweet potatoes onto her plate. "They used to take jump ropes and tie me to my bed while I was sleeping. One time I woke up in the middle of the night and I had to go to the bathroom so bad but I couldn't get out of bed. They had me tied over my shoulders and my knees—must've used four or five ropes, all tied together. And I couldn't even make it out and my goodness, they just laughed." With the turban she looks like something from a children's picture book—Ali Baba, Scheherazade, ink bleeding, blurred. "Did you do things like that to your little sister?" Nana has stopped eating. She watches Louise as though she's waiting for something ugly.

"No—God no. I mean, we—my sister and I weren't close," I say, and as soon as these words leave my mouth I'm struck by their absurdity, and their truth. Louise gives no sign of having heard.

"That wasn't the worst thing they did," she says. "We had a dog run in the backyard—"

"Louise," Nana says, "why don't you take the ice cream out to soften? I don't think those pies are warm enough to do the trick anymore." She pulls her cigarettes from a sweater pocket, cellophane crackling, and shakes one from the wrinkled pack. Louise makes no move toward the freezer.

"What does your sister do?" she says, and for a moment I'm confused. The bottle of wine is empty, the table a ruin. *She didn't do anything,* I think. *She stayed away from me, mostly, or watched from our bedroom window, and I returned the favor. She was angry most of the time, and I don't know if that's true anymore.*

"She studies, I guess," I say. "She's graduating from college this year."

Louise's smile fills the kitchen, dazzling, predatory. "College," she says. "I guess so. I guess that's right. Toby took some classes. Up the highway, about a half-hour away. He loved it—said those teachers were the funniest he'd ever had. Said they were worth twice what he was paying—remember, Nana? Those teachers?"

The tape has been on an endless loop, a whir and click to signal the end of one side before the bells and fiddles start up again, as bright as the fluorescent light over our heads. Nana taps ash into a saucer. Her son belonged to someone else when he died, and one long drag of her cigarette would burn my throat clean. I want to watch her, to catalog her slow careful movements and the thin lines around her mouth, evidence of a life I know nothing about, long years in this house, this town and other places, but I cannot keep my eyes from Louise for longer than a second or two before they're drawn back again—I've never felt vertigo but I think this is what it must be like, this tunnel vision, Louise's wide face at the center of it and my hands perilously close to reaching for her like a life raft, like a lover, while my feet tingle in my high-heeled boots and the floor slopes down and away from them into someplace dark.

"It must be so hard for you both," I say, and my voice is silk, vulgar, low and soothing. "I can't imagine."

Nana crushes the cigarette out and looks at me, eyes dry and watchful. She waits only a second before opening her mouth but Louise stands, scraping her chair along the linoleum. "How about those pies?" she says, wiping her hands on her napkin. "I'll just put the slices in the microwave and the ice cream'll melt fine." She begins to stack plates, transfer them to the sink. I stand to help and Nana says, "Martha, why don't you grab that bottle of bourbon and some fresh glasses? Put it on the table."

I do this, and she pours a few fingers into her glass and mine. She pulls another cigarette from her pack but lays it on the table, unlit. "No more than any other day," she says. She smiles at me, and in the bright light of the kitchen her skin is almost translucent, covering nothing but a beating heart.

———

It's dark by the time I get home, and it seems to have gotten warmer. A gray nimbus glows around the light at the end of the block and for a moment I'm confused; it seems too dark too early. Louise has sent me off with two covered plates, heavy with food, enough for me and someone else. Enough for me, for the next few days. I put them in the refrigerator and bring a bottle of wine, a glass, and the phone to the living room. Three messages blinking. I erase them without listening and pour a glass of wine. I consider driving to the convenience store for a pack of cigarettes—I think about this carefully, from every angle. I think about this as I dial my parents' number, as I click the television on and mute it.

"Mom. Merry Christmas."

"Martha! We've been trying to call you. Where were you? Did you eat? Your father's right here—Joseph, pick up the other line. Merry Christmas, honey. Everyone was asking about you."

"I was next door. I spent the day with the neighbors, I just walked in the door."

"Did you go to church?" There's a click and my father's voice. "Hey, little girl," he says.

"Hi, Daddy. I went this morning. I missed you," I say, and out of the lie spins a truth I'm never sure of. I picture them in separate rooms, the short sides of a triangle that meet in this house they've never seen, wires strung high between us for a thousand miles.

"Everyone asked about you," my mother says again. "Charlie and Rose Morelli had all the kids over, and the grandkids are so big— but Charlie doesn't look so good. And you should see Marie—"

"How are you, little girl?" my father says. A woman on the television is modeling a sweater like Nana's. The price has been reduced over and over; numbers on the side of the screen are crossed out and flashing.

"I'm fine." I pour more wine into the glass.

"Did you get the package?" my mother says. "Your father took it to the post office Monday."

"Not yet," I say. "But mail's slow down here—"

"I told you we should've sent it earlier! You should've had it there last Friday—"

"Mom, don't worry about it. I'll let you know when it comes, okay?" I'm listening and I should be able to hear traffic, music, something to fill the space between the phones my parents are holding. The woman in the sweater is gone from the screen and in her place is a little girl in a swingy red coat and patent shoes, her legs like candy canes. She twirls slowly, her arms out, a music box ballerina winding down.

"Are you having anyone over tonight?" There is no reason for me to ask this. Their house is as still as mine.

"Oh no," my mother says. "Everyone was tired today. I just got the dishes all put away and my nightgown on."

"Is Carly around?" Another glass. The little girl unbuttons the coat. It's lined with something that looks like silk.

"She went out a while ago. Where'd they go, Anne?"

My mother sniffs. "Probably some bar. I don't know why anyone would want to go to a bar on Christmas. I didn't even think they'd be open."

"Sure they're open," I say. "They do pretty good business, too, from what I gather."

"I can't imagine such a thing," she says. "I'd think that would be the last place anyone would want to be on Christmas."

She has no idea—a bar is the safest place to be on a holiday. There's no tension, no chance of a drunken fight. Everyone there has left all that at home and the air is heavy and warm. When people's eyes meet—and they meet only by accident—they smile, if they can, and if they can't it's no matter. Their gaze is direct and clear and kind.

"Tell her to call me," I say. "Not too late. But I'll be around tomorrow night."

"What's too late?" my mother says. The woman with the poinsettia sweater reappears on the stage and takes the little girl's hand. They swing arms as though they're strolling through a park but their feet move only slightly, left, then right, and left again. The little girl's arm is raised at an awkward angle and I think of starfish.

Twenty-two. Twenty-two is too late for everything. I didn't know this until now, until too late.

"Just tell her she can call me tomorrow. If she's around. I think I need to go now—I hear carolers outside."

"I love you," my father says, and my mother. I tell them the same. I hang up the phone and take my glass and a blanket outside, warmer even than when I came in but still as death. I imagine carolers moving in a woolly group, mittens and sheet music and candy canes. They would arrange themselves around the porch steps and their voices would lift into stars. I've never seen carolers in my life. Where do such things happen? The sky holds its breath.

———

The last thing I do before Christmas ends is call Edward. At eleven-thirty I stand in the bathroom, the light bright and wrong, and brush my hair, line and fill in my lips with red and blot them on a tissue, a ghost kiss. At eleven-forty-five I'm ready—no excuse necessary for this, no reason, it's Christmas, O holy night, good will toward men, I think, and I am filled with it, that or something close. My hands are shaking and I run cold water over them and I think of everything I will say, every way I will apologize to him for these months that I've been gone and the months before when I was there; I will bathe him cleaner than I ever did. My hands are cold and smooth. At twenty-two I would have followed him across a desert and imagined the sand was sugar, white and melting, sweet on my skin and in my eyes.

I think: I will drive to see him, hide myself in his bed away from anyplace I could call home and tell him anything he wants to hear. *Any, any*—so easy to say, even easier to think, and so I do, because to do this is to *refuse* the possibility of thought and what could be easier than that? To promise what I don't know, to lie on cool sheets and wait to be surprised by what my mouth offers, what gifts, what magic? I will unspool myself like barbed wire, not wait for him to ask, I will let him twist me back into what I should have been all along. *Make me a mother*, I think, *make me a wife, give me what I've never wanted, fill my mouth with flesh and sew my eyes closed.* And I will let him.

The phone rings, twice, four times, six; the answering machine picks up and I listen to his voice telling me to speak and my red mouth opens but nothing comes, no promises, no lies; I listen to the whir of tape and the click of a disconnected line and the high whine of space, the only sound for miles.

Through my fault through my fault through my most grievous fault.

IN MY BED, WESLEY SHIVERS beneath the blankets, he hoards them. He pulls on the edges at a diagonal so that my foot is exposed, and in the flickering candlelight the white of it makes me think of a root, something meant to be underground.

He is nothing like the boys I knew. He sees only what is in front of him, he doesn't look for anything more. Dark hair, green eyes, silence.

"Can we close the window?" he says. "It's freezing in here."

I close the window all but an inch. He wants nothing from me that I can't give. He has a wife already, he has dozens of children in the daytime. He is nothing like Edward. I could turn my back on Wesley with no fear of what might happen.

"It's late," he says. His wife is away, visiting family. It's just after New Year's. It isn't late at all.

"School tomorrow?"

"Faculty meetings. All day." He stretches his arm over my pillow, his hand just touching my head. "Then the kids are back the day after. It's worse than the end of summer, this time of year. For them, I mean. For us, everyone says it's like never being gone. A few weeks."

He goes on, he speaks. He tells me about the other teachers, and it's so easy to half-listen, to let my vision settle and blur at a point over his shoulder while the names wash over me, people I don't know, have no intention of knowing. He tells me about them in such a way that I know he will eventually tell me more, that this will not be the last conversation we have here, like this one or any other. He lies in my bed as though he's been in it before.

". . . so they kicked him out. Called the parents and that was it. Martha?"

His face is wide and soft at the jaw. The stubble on his chin is sparse, patchy.

"Where'd you go?" he says. His hand falls to my shoulder and rests there.

"Is this going to happen again?" I say. "I think we should decide now."

He came into the store before closing. I'd sent the girls home early. He told me he wanted to have a drink with me and he didn't suggest going out to a bar. I hadn't seen him for weeks, hadn't thought about him or wondered where he'd been.

"Decide?" he says. "Do we need to do that? I thought—" He waits for me to interrupt him. I don't. I have patience. There are no phone calls for me to receive somewhere else, no lights to turn on for the neighbors.

"I didn't think there was anything to decide." He lifts his hand from my shoulder for only a moment before letting it fall back. "I want to see you again."

You want to fuck me again. Me, I closed my eyes.

"Okay. That's fine. Then we should be clear, I think."

"Jesus, Martha." He sits up, the pillow longways behind him. He tugs at the covers, and suddenly things are not so easy. "I thought we were having a good time," he says, a little boy who's been scolded. I'm all out of understanding.

"You're missing my point," I say. "I don't want there to be confusion. We'll see each other. But I'm not going to call you, and we're not going to make any plans. Can you live with that?"

He is immobile, but I can almost feel the humming beneath his skin, the awareness of time, minutes ticking, the phone in his house ringing, a long-distance call. And I wonder at the way skin against skin can play tricks on a clock, the way time can fill a body: slow minutes into hours that bleed out too fast to catch.

"I have to go," he says, throws the blankets back and reaches for his clothes on the floor. I am suddenly contrite.

"I'm sorry," I say. "I didn't mean that the way it sounded. Wesley." He's got his boxers and one sock on. His back is freckled. "I only meant that it's better for you to gauge things. Do you see? Your wife," I say. It's the first time I've said these two words to him outside of the store. They taste different in my mouth, sweeter, and I think of Louise's Christmas punch. He gets the other sock on and sits up. When I touch his back I can feel gooseflesh, but I am so warm.

"This is hard for me," he says, and turns to look me in the face. What he means is that it must be easy for me, and it is, but not for the reason he imagines. I've never done this before. "I'm not upset with you, I just don't want to leave."

His car is parked in my driveway. No one on my street would know his car—no students, or parents. He came in through the front door. Everyone here is old, except for Louise, and he doesn't know about Louise. He thinks he is safe.

He leans over to kiss me and I let him. "I *will* call you," he says. "Next weekend. My wife doesn't get home until Sunday."

His wife. I think of Connie, Connie years ago in cutoffs and a shirt I loaned her, a size too small, eyes turned up to the ceiling of my bedroom while I brushed mascara on her lashes. I will never tell her about this.

He's dressed. I put a robe on and follow him to the front door, open it. The air is warmer than January has any right to be.

"How'd you find this place?" he says. "There're nicer neighborhoods, Martha. Do you have a lease?"

"It's fine here," I tell him.

"When you're ready to buy, let me know. You want something nice. You want somewhere with people around. No one even has their lights on." He touches my face with the flat of his cold hand.

"Have a good night," I say to him, the way I'd say it to anyone leaving the store.

"I did," he says, and steps out onto the porch, flipping his keys in his hand.

I close and lock the door before he's in his car. I wait behind it, listening to the engine catch, the crunch of gravel as he backs out. In here, time is smoothed out, constant again, no more noteworthy than a pulse in a wrist. For him I think it still must be skittering, the dashboard clock winking green as he rolls silently through stop signs toward his phone. I tie my robe more tightly and collect a broom and dustpan, furniture polish and old towels, and begin to clean the house.

———

Carly calls me more over the next week than she ever has. She's staying in Baltimore until the day before classes start again, something else she's never done before, and I imagine how happy our parents must be, thinking this is for a reason it is not. Her voice on the phone is half-frantic, the words tumbling out until they come quivering to rest at a silence that I am meant to fill. Questions, I think—Edward's eyes, his hair, the sound of his voice and the things he says to her, the smell of him. She tells me just enough to leave space for me to ask these things.

But I have never asked her such things, about anyone. I have watched her from distances and left it at that, and there is nothing in me now that could find a way to close the space.

And besides, I know all the answers.

"He's taking me out to dinner tomorrow night," she says. "Sotto Sopra. And I didn't really bring any clothes with me for that, you know? I think I might go shopping tomorrow—what do you think? A skirt? Have you been there?"

No. And he would have been the last person to take me there.

"Just wear a nice pair of pants," I say. "Get a sweater or something. And wear jewelry."

"Did I tell you about the earrings he got me?"

I can picture them: something I would sell. My jaw aches— I've been grinding my teeth in my sleep. When I did this in his bed he would wake me, hand me a glass of water.

"You told me," I say.

"Those, do you think? Or something else?"

A collar and leash, I think. *A choke-chain with a leather grip. Something tasteful—he's not showy.* I open my mouth wide, suck at my cheeks.

"Martha?"

"I don't know, Carly. It depends. But do something with your hair, okay? Mom has some old hot rollers somewhere."

There's something vulgar about all this, this chattering nonsense with neither history nor purpose tricked out like something real, something *true,* an old whore in clotted pink lipstick.

"What's wrong with my hair?" she says. Something new again—she would have ignored a comment like this from me in the past.

"Nothing's *wrong* with it." Her hair is beautiful. "But maybe put it in rollers and spritz it with some hairspray. Then comb it out. Nothing huge," I tell her. "Just something a little different from the way he's seen you before." I press my fingers under my chin, feeling for damage. She says nothing. I can hear sirens behind her.

"You're not in the bedroom, are you?" I say. The windows there look out onto the back alley.

"Living room." No one we knew ever used their living rooms. Ours is on the street level of the house; the kitchen and den and back door are in the basement. There's an off-white sofa where she is and new blue armchairs. The sirens fade, and there's nothing more.

"Carly, I didn't mean that to be nasty," I say.

"He wants to pick me up here. And I can't picture what Mom and Dad'll do when they see him. He's a lot older, Martha."

Not so much, I think. He'll charm them. He'll be wearing a jacket and good shoes. He'll drink a glass of wine with them. *Whatever you do, don't stand there like you used to. Don't run your fingers through your hair until it hangs in strings, don't rock back on your shoes. Buy a pair of heels tomorrow, buy a skirt, cut your hair. Put on lipstick and pretend you're someone else if you have to. Not our mother, not me. Someone close to perfect. He's waiting for that.*

"You know," I say, "if I were you I'd be more worried about the fact that you met him in a bar."

"Fuck you, Martha."

I sigh. "I'm kidding. You'll be fine. Just open the door, introduce them, and get out of there as soon as you can." *Let him open the car door for you, let him pull out your chair at the restaurant. Go for drinks after dinner if he wants to, but nothing more than that.*

"I have to go," she says. "Mom's coming upstairs. You don't want to talk to her, do you?"

"Not necessary."

We say our good-byes. It's early yet, not quite nine on a Monday night. The house is spotless, refrigerator stocked for the week and the laundry done. Tomorrow I will put my face back on, open the store and watch the street, the cars that line up two or three deep at the stoplight at the corner. At eleven-thirty or so I can watch the glass door of the diner, the men in suits trickling through it in twos and threes—no one seems to eat alone. At three Kerry will come in, curly hair held back with an elastic, throw her backpack on the floor of the tiny back room and unlock a case of barrettes. She'll take a full ten minutes to decide which one to wear. When she's settled I'll cross the street myself and order a hamburger to take back with me, bun sopping with grilled onions and mayonnaise. This is food I would never have eaten.

I'm standing in the bathroom, running water over my hands until it scalds when the phone rings again, and even before I answer I can hear Edward's voice, saying he's tired of this, whatever it is; ready to tell me that my sister was a game, a mistake; ready to purr any cruel thing into my ear because it's time, the holidays and all their sad excuses are over—we're back to ourselves, now, ugly and worn, and I'm ready to hear it, whatever it is. I pick up the phone, and the sound of Wesley's voice is like milk.

"What are you doing?" he says. He assumes I'll know his voice, and the fact that I do is a cold pick in my heart.

"I was washing my hands." This is true, or close enough, but I have enough in me to regret saying it. "I cleaned the house." No better. "I do it every Monday night. Makes going to work easier." *I'm sorry*, I think.

"Look, if you don't want to do this—" And this time I do interrupt him, I say the thing he wants to hear, and I tell myself that it's true even so. I say to him, "Wesley, I do. If you call me, I'll be here."

He says he will, tomorrow night after his faculty meeting, and I hang up the phone, my hands red and puffy. I am not lonely, I tell myself. This is not what lonely feels like, this thrumming heat. Lonely is for people whose lives have nothing to do with mine.

I never asked my mother why she waited so long to marry my father, and I never asked her why she stopped waiting for the other one.

I run the hot water full force in the bathroom sink and tie my hair back. When the bowl is full and steaming I drop a clean washcloth into it, fish it out with the tips of my fingers, fold it in half and bring it to my face. Edward is meeting my parents tomorrow night—something I would never let him do. When the washcloth begins to cool I drop it into the sink and press it to my face again. Water runs and drips from my elbows to the clean floor. My eyelids burn, my lips, but neither as much as my fingers do—strange that these parts of me, rarely touched now, are more resilient than my hands. My fingertips are ridged and callused, bitten by fine wire and pricked. An occupational hazard.

In a movie, now, something would happen. But this is my life, one moment of it, and nothing does—the phone is silent, the door knocker still, and the space I occupy is a small one. It's as quick as that, I think: the click of receiver into cradle and the beginning of things is over, the narrow door opened into a new room, big enough to get lost in. *If you call me, I'll be here*—I don't know where *here* is.

THE SUMMER AFTER WE graduated from high school, Sticky Bucara killed April Miller. We hadn't grown up with her. She'd moved back to the neighborhood the year before with her mother, after her parents' divorce. My mother remembered April's mother, though she remembered her as Patsy Mancuso. They'd gone through high school together.

April was blond and quiet and called Sticky *Frank*—she was the only girl who did. The rest of us remembered the summers with the ice cream truck, the melting Popsicles striped as blue as his eyes, and none of us could let the name go. He hated us all a little for this.

Don told Connie and me that Sticky would go to bars in Fell's Point where he knew the bouncers and sit by the DJ's booth to drink. Women were constantly going to the booth to make requests—it was a better spot to meet them than the bar, or a table by the door, he said. On the rare occasions that Sticky came to parties he told the boys stories about this, the time he spent in clubs that none of us went to, but he was always alone. He was going to Georgetown University in the fall, which may as well have been the moon.

But April. She was beautiful, pure gold. She came at the beginning of senior year and managed to negotiate the quagmire of us all like an egret. When we saw her and her mother in church my mother would say to me *Ask her over. She must be lonely. Ask her to dinner sometime—it would mean a lot to me.*

She wasn't lonely, and I never asked her to dinner. I rarely spoke to her at school because we had no classes together, but when I saw her on weekends she was completely at ease, standing with a group of girls or sitting with a boy on either side of her. I was in awe of her composure—she was the first person I'd met who had what I thought was *poise*—and it was only after I'd talked with her more than a few times that I came to understand the source of this. April Miller wasn't particularly bright. She spoke little, smiled often, nodded in agreement in any conversation. If anyone else had figured out the reason for these things, I didn't know about it. I never heard a bad word against her. By spring, Sticky had started coming to every party, and when he sat next to April or offered her a drink from his monogrammed flask the other boys would float away, quiet as smoke.

I watched him. There was no reason for me to be subtle about it—no one knew that I had ever gone to a bedroom with him and failed at what I did so easily with others. I thought of it this way. And it amazes me now that none of us saw how beautiful he had become—finer than the other boys. In the bedroom with him I hadn't seen it. His face was no different from the rest of them.

His family had money. In the fifth grade his mother planned a birthday party for him and invited the whole class, thirty ten-year-olds in a steak restaurant downtown. She reserved the banquet room for lunch on a Saturday. I remember the dress I wore, plaid with ribbons at the collar and hem. Other birthday parties were thrown in basements, balloons taped to doorjambs and bags of gum and plastic toys as favors.

In the restaurant, there were folded cards with our names on them at the place settings. We were seated alphabetically. Waiters poured ice water into heavy goblets, splashing the tablecloth. I couldn't imagine being so cavalier at home. We were served salads with creamy dressing and crackers in cellophane wrappers, and by the time the waiters brought trays of Shirley Temples the boys had begun flicking the balled-up cellophane at one another and letting ice cubes fall out of their mouths. Mrs. Bucara, who sat at a small table with her husband, said *Now everyone, when you've finished the salads put the forks on your plates.* But we knew enough to do that.

We were cutting into the tiny steaks and watching the blood pool onto our plates when Sticky began to choke. His feet hammered the legs of the chair until it tipped back, spilling him onto the floor, and the staff came rushing *Is he epileptic Is it a seizure My sister has seizures Stand back I know what to do* but it was a piece of meat lodged high in his windpipe, his grown-up tie splattered with Shirley Temple and a lettuce leaf stuck to his pants. His mother was on her feet and then on her knees on the floor next to him *Sweet Jesus my baby Frankie Jesus* and then his father was there, pulling him up, wrapping his arms under his ribcage and Sticky flipped forward like a puppet and began to gasp, great whistling breaths, the piece of meat out of him, somewhere on the swirled pile rug.

We were silent, all of us. Sticky sobbed in rage, flailing against his mother, all but hidden beneath the curve of her back, her blouse pulled clear of her skirt. I could see the beige silk of her slip. The presents were stacked on a table in a corner of the room. None of our parents were coming to get us for another two hours.

They came anyway. I don't know how Mr. Bucara arranged it, but within fifteen minutes cars began to pull up at the awning of the restaurant. The waiters were clearing our barely touched plates away, and as we left in twos and threes each of us received a piece of birthday cake, frosted green and blue and wrapped in cellophane. My mother came for Connie and me. We climbed into the backseat and she turned to us, her face blotchy with panic—*Is he all right? What happened? He'll be all right, won't he?*—and my God, we began to laugh. We fell against each other in our stiff dresses and let the pieces of cake drop to the seat of the car. My mother's mouth tightened and we didn't stop. He was fine. The steak was too bloody to eat and he was fine. I imagined his father loading the presents into the trunk of their car, and after my mother dropped Connie off she turned and caught me across the cheek with the back of her hand. *You think this is funny? That poor woman! When we get home I want you up in your room. And stay there.*

April knew none of this. In the hall at school she and Sticky would linger, not touching, until the last bell rang, and April went into the classroom across the hall and Sticky came into ours, took the desk across from mine. *Please take your sunglasses off, Mr. Bucara,* the nun would say, and Sticky slid them into his shirt pocket, smiling at the floor.

He spoke to me as though I knew nothing about him, as though he had never led me up carpeted stairs by the hand, the noise below us fading with every step. To say that I wanted him then would be wrong: what I wanted was an undoing to things, a fast trip back that would erase bedrooms and steak restaurants and ice cream trucks and make him no different from the rest of them, make him as coarse and silly and manageable as the rest of them, as *small* as the rest of them. He was all these things to April. He was another prize, no more.

That summer after graduation was like any other—we worked to make it so. We talked on the phone for no reason and met in small groups in Patterson Park to figure out what to do for the rest of the night. We said little about what would happen in the fall and I felt like a ghost, a liar.

Sticky and April weren't sleeping together. I knew this to be true because we hadn't heard otherwise. She wanted to marry him—I knew this to be true because I *had* heard it, we all had, from the girls April spent her time with when she wasn't with Sticky. She spoke to them of his visits home before he'd even begun packing to leave, desperation or stupid faith in her voice or a combination of the two. If Sticky had changed his mind, decided not to go, she would never have tried to convince him otherwise.

There was a party the night she died, dozens of us crowded into someone's backyard. It was too hot to be inside and so we sat on the back steps or crouched around them, trying to be quiet enough that the neighbors wouldn't complain. I remember the dress April was wearing, white and dotted with flowers, and I remember how pretty she looked. It was nothing I would have worn. She was drunk, and loud—Sticky was feeding her from his flask. He held it to her mouth and she wrapped both hands around his, smiling around the neck of it.

They left early, his hand on the small of her back, steering her down the narrow back sidewalk. There was a party in her old neighborhood, ten miles out of the city. She wanted Sticky—*Frank*—to meet her friends.

I can picture the rest: Sticky tucks her into his father's car, gives her the flask to hold while he drives. He doesn't swerve—

I'd only ever seen him drunk once. He drives them out of the city and her eyes are half-closed, head falling to her shoulder, and she laughs, a laugh like water, like rain. She rolls the window down when they get onto the highway and puts her arm out, lets her hand float in the rushing dark. He takes the exit and she has to give him directions from there, point him down narrow roads, still laughing, her breath hot and sweet. It's June, eleven-thirty on a Tuesday night, she's drunk enough to fuck and he's sober enough to do it, but they're still in the car, still trying to get to the place they're going, three missed turns behind them.

What now, smart girl? I imagine him saying, and she reaches over to unzip his pants and take him in her hand, or her mouth, and Frank Bucara's blue eyes close for one moment too long, and the car goes through a guardrail and flips into a ditch.

At least part of this is true—the car was in the grass, on its side, April some distance away. Sticky was wearing his seat belt. It's not strictly true that God looks after drunks and little children—April Miller was both of those things that night. Sticky was not even knocked unconscious. He was taken to the hospital for observation and released the next day. April was buried in a cemetery by her old house, near the place they were going that night, near where Connie and Don live now. The rest of the summer passed without incident. There was a party at the end of August, quiet for its size, and that was all.

———

I should know what happened to Sticky, but I don't. He disappeared in a way the rest of them didn't. I would run into the others occasionally, then less and less frequently, a gradual fade that either sped up or slowed down as time passed, depending on how you look at it. And eventually the easiest thing to do if I saw them was to duck away, or hide my face until they'd passed. I stopped going to places they might be. I went with Edward to the places he knew, ones I'd never gone to before, and when he introduced me to his friends I was happy enough. But I never saw Sticky. He had taken himself somewhere else.

I imagine Sticky with a boat, in a place like Annapolis, closer to home than I am now but safer all the same. I picture him in a white shirt, tanned arms and face, his hair shot through with gold. When he takes his watch off at night there's a white band of skin around his wrist. He introduces himself as Frank and there's no one who knows enough to disagree. I imagine too that if he thinks of April he thinks of her as something that happened to someone else, pale and shadowy, insubstantial—which is true, in its way.

But mostly when I think of him now I think of the night I followed him up the stairs and into someone else's bedroom. I remember being on top of him and wanting to say his name, to lean into his mouth and breathe magic into it, breathe us both away from that house in the middle of everything we'd known. His name—*names*—I said neither. When he came out of the bathroom after, we looked at one another and saw nothing that could save us.

I grieve for him, not April. When I think of that night in the car I think of him opening his eyes to see the passenger seat empty, the open window facing up into the hot stars, headlights dumb and white, illuminating nothing. I imagine him crawling out to lie in the grass like a child and stare up into the night sky.

And I think of his mother, who still has her son, her little boy with blue eyes. She wasn't there to see him in the car that night. What she must have seen was him at ten years old, heels beating a happy rhythm into the carpet of a restaurant, hands clawing at his own throat as though to open it up. She must have been happy when she thought of this, because it was not the end of the story, not even the middle.

He left the bedroom before me, closed the door behind him. I straightened my shirt and combed my hair with a brush I found on the dresser. There were photographs there, on the dresser and wedged into the frame of the mirror, some taken in the cafeteria at school and some at other parties, groups of three and five and ten in our white school shirts or bright weekend clothes, arms around one another, mouths open, teeth bared.

I put lipstick on and went downstairs. Connie and Don were gone, the music still thumping, the television on but muted. On the screen a man in leather pants screamed silently into a microphone. Sticky was sprawled in front of it, his head propped against the sofa, legs resting over someone's back. I dug my jacket from a pile in the corner and felt a hand on my wrist, gripping hard enough to hurt.

"You leaving?" Sticky said. I pulled my hand away and slid through a knot of people to the back door. At the alley I heard the door swing open behind me.

"Hey," he said. He was unsteady on his feet. I waited. I pulled my jacket tighter around me. Five blocks home—my father would be asleep on the couch, my mother asleep in their bed, Carly awake in the half-light of our bedroom window.

He took a step down, his hand on the wooden railing. "If you think—" He staggered, caught himself. "It's all the same, Martha."

This was what I was afraid of.

So WHAT ARE THE THINGS a person can map her life by? Births, deaths—I'm lucky. Neither has come close enough to touch. Something must come after something else—spring follows winter, for instance. But winter here is over before it ever takes hold. It's February and the moon is blurry in the mild sky, a smudged pearl. You could roll it in your palms, soft and forgiving. But January is done, and that's something.

Wesley and I have slept together nine times. The fact that I know this, that the number is so easily retrievable, makes me feel like a child again. I kept a page in the back of my diary where I listed the kisses I'd had—the boys, the places. At a certain point I stopped.

Wesley and I are on a date—or what might be called a date, in another circumstance. But it has all the trappings of one. He picked me up in his car and we drove to the outskirts of a town about five miles north up the highway, the same last five miles I drove to get here. He parked in the lot of a restaurant called Fagin's and opened the car door for me, followed me into the tiny vestibule.

Fagin's is fancy, or trying to be. There are banquettes with high curved backs along the walls of the dining room, upholstered in fabric made to look like tapestry, and white tablecloths with dark green napkins folded into goblets. But there's no one here—a few couples eating silently at the back of the room, a man with a briefcase on the floor next to him and papers spread over his table, a salad pushed to the side. Wesley guides me into the bar. He pulls a stool out for me and I sit.

"A glass of cabernet, and a Heineken," he tells the bartender, who nods. I pull a pack of cigarettes from my purse.

"I didn't know you smoked," he says.

"I don't. I used to. If it bothers you—"

"Not at all." He smiles. "I just didn't know. I don't know much about you, I guess." The bartender sets our drinks in front of us and I tap a cigarette out of the pack. "That's why I wanted to take you out," he says. "It doesn't seem right."

His wife is out of town again, visiting her family in St. Louis. I know this about her, where she's from, and I can't begin to imagine how he thinks that knowing more about me will make this right. I try to think of something that *would* make it right, any small thing—that I could love him, for instance. I take a sip of my wine and light the cigarette and as soon as the smoke is in my lungs my head swims. This is not enough. I am as far from love as it's possible to be.

————

For the next hour he tells me about his wife. I ask him to do this. I light one cigarette off the end of the last and drink two glasses of wine for every one of his beers, and listen, and the listening grows harder. I can picture his wife, a little girl, long hair in ribbons, shoes clipping the marble floors of her family's house, a huge house with stained-glass transom windows. "What's a transom window?" I ask him, and motion for the bartender.

More people come in. The hostess seats them, her black padded shoes noiseless, ponytail brushing the back of her bow tie. Every surface here is designed to muffle sound, to suck human voices into a senseless hum. He tells me about her so easily, so artlessly, my heart breaks a little for him. He has no idea that this is not what's supposed to be done, that the two of us sitting here depends on nothing but secrets. Even I know this much.

"She majored in art history," he says. "Her father was a collector. So it's hard for her down here—I'm at school most of the time, there's not a lot for her to do—"

The bartender empties my ashtray when he brings another glass of wine. Wesley pauses while he does this, sips from his beer and smiles at him. The bartender's face is inscrutable, and I wonder what I am looking for in it.

"Go on," I say to Wesley. "What else?"

He is happy to oblige. In St. Louis, she worked in a gallery next to the restaurant where he sometimes drank. She and the owner would come in after closing.

"She looked like she worked in a place like that. Nice clothes, you know, those little glasses with the wire rims. But she didn't really take care of her hands—I noticed that. Never polished her nails or anything. I thought that was strange. Not like yours," he says, and reaches for one of them. I pull it into my lap.

"What else?" I say. He would talk all night if I asked him to. The bartender returns and asks if he can bring menus. He's diplomatic. I need to use the bathroom but I don't trust my legs. With Edward, it was never like this. No matter how much we drank I was lucid, the edges of things sharp and humming, the light always just bright enough to see what needed to be seen and nothing more.

Listen, I want to say to him, *I'm sorry. I'm sorry nine times over.* One more time and I could make it an even decade on the rosary beads in the bottom of my jewelry box. I used to wear them around my neck as a little girl, put a scarf over my head and pretend to be a nun. I climbed up on my mother's silky lap like that, and she asked me if I wouldn't rather have her earrings, her lipstick and dark glasses. Those came later.

The bartender comes back with a plate of stuffed mushrooms and two sets of silverware wrapped in green napkins. I fork one into my mouth and remember that I hate mushrooms. I don't tell Wesley this.

"So she visits her family a lot. I used to go with her but I got tired of it—she wanted to stay for long weekends and I couldn't, and she spent most of the time with her sister anyway—"

Her sister. What's her sister like, I want to ask, is she younger? Is she beautiful in a way your wife is not? Could you just as easily be sitting next to her right now, in a half-empty restaurant in a town close by, but far enough? These are important questions. They are important because every triangle has three sides— yours, hers, and the truth's. Wait—I'm mixing my metaphors. These questions are important because I am alone. I am here because I am alone. Nine nights, the Trinity tripled, cubed. Make it an even ten and put it away, next to the rosary and my mother's lovely narrow skirts, out of sight but impossible to forget. You will not be impossible to forget.

He eats the mushrooms, I force another down. Before long there's only one left on the plate, and it will sit there until the bartender takes it away because Wesley would never eat the last of anything, I know this, and I am sorry for every kind thought I haven't had about him.

"She's a good person," he says. His napkin is folded neatly by the plate. "I don't want you to think I'm trying to justify this—"

You should, I think. You should be trying to justify it. You should because I have given this privilege over to you, this right of interpretation; I have shirked my responsibilities and burned my bridges with cold fire and silence and none of it is golden.

Behind me there's a whisper of cold air, movement and some sweet perfume I haven't smelled since my grandmother died—My Sin, or Shalimar. A couple sits across the bar from us and the woman is young, too young to be wearing a perfume like that, I think. She shrugs out of her coat and her shirt is a rough plaid, shapeless. With that perfume she should have heavy silk draped over her shoulders and streaks of silver in her hair. The man with her asks the bartender for two glasses of chardonnay—I don't actually hear this, but I see the bartender pour. He sets the glasses on the bar and they pick them up immediately, touch the bowls and kiss. *Congratulations*, I think. I'm so tired.

"Do you know them?" Wesley says. "I came here because I thought we wouldn't see anyone—"

You thought right, but you didn't need to. We could be sitting in the diner in the middle of town and I wouldn't know anyone. That's the beauty of this—it's what I wanted.

I excuse myself to use the restroom. It's on the other side of the bar and so I have to walk past this couple and their chardonnay. Wesley hands me my purse from the floor under his stool and I keep my eyes on them, their faces flickering above the squat cut-glass candle holders, the rest of the room a haze. When I pass behind their chairs the purse slides from my fingers and spills onto the floor, keys and lipstick and wallet scattering. A gift, a prayer answered.

Her shoes are brown leather, thick-soled, the laces wound into something between a knot and a bow. Red and white socks, a fraying checkerboard. The man leans over and I wave him away, collect my things and fit them back into the purse before Wesley can come to help and I breathe her in. The sweet blue smell of her is everywhere.

"Did you get everything?" she says when I stand. I raise my purse, close it and smile. "I never carry them," she says. "I was always losing them."

Wesley is watching us and before I can stop myself my hand is on her forearm and I'm leaning into the blue air around her. "My grandmother wore that perfume, I haven't smelled it in so long but when you came in I remembered."

Her arm stiffens under my hand and I step back.

In Baltimore there are little girls and then there are wives but nothing in between. There are no wives who are not mothers within a year or two. No map, no need for directions; one way, straight and sure, no one could get lost.

"That's nice," she says to me.

Is it? Tell me. Because I need to know. Because somehow, as strange as it may seem, I disappeared in all of that, fell off the ride into a small place, unmapped but with a view. I could still see. Here, the trees go on. They hide everything beneath them, and when I look out my window the houses are closed boxes, sealed up, done waiting. What is there to wait for? A husband. I have one now who isn't mine.

"Are you all right?" the man says to me. They glance at one another, and then at Wesley, over their chardonnay. He's watching.

"No, I'm fine. Fine. We were just getting ready to leave."

I go back around the bar and stand behind Wesley's stool. "Are we paid up?" I say.

"The bathroom——" he says.

"Let's just go. Let's pay and go. Here." I pull money from my purse and lay it on the bar. "I'll wait for you outside." I'm out the door before he can give the money back and the parking lot is bright, no light but the moon. I can't remember which car is his. He'll pay cash, no receipt that way. I know at least this little bit.

There's the two-lane we came in on, sandy shoulders, on the other side a few yards of scrubby grass and then the beginning of the trees. No cars coming, so I cross and walk a few steps back toward the highway, the intersection, the four stop signs. My coat is almost too warm. The quiet is something I'm not used to yet. Every small sound carries farther than it should—a car a few miles behind me, the door of the restaurant opening. Wesley's on the steps, looking over the parking lot, and I jog back over. I'm on my way to sober and not ready to be.

"What were you doing?" he says, puts his arm around me and begins to walk to the car. It's small and brown, Japanese. On the back seat is a pile of clothes.

"Just looking," I say.

He stands over me, holding the door open. "At what?"

"Nothing much, apparently." He draws back slightly and I'm sorry. "Nothing," I say again. "Really. Do you mind if I sleep on the way back?" Pain is settling behind my eyes and I wish for a glass of water. He gets in and starts the car.

"You can put the seat down. Here." He reaches over me to pull a lever and I push back, tuck the seat belt under my arm. I turn my head and see that the clothing on the back seat is a sweater, crumpled under my headrest now.

"What's this?" I shake it open. A pale cardigan with rounded pearl buttons, softer than anything I own. Cashmere. "What color is it?"

"Martha," he says. The car rolls to a stop and I can hear the turn signal. *Why bother?* I think. *For what?*

"It's Pamela's," he says, and takes it from my hands, lets it fall behind me.

Pamela. I consider this. Cashmere sweaters and transom win-
dows, a sister. Just like me, I think, and begin to laugh, eyes
closed, and we roll on.

"Are you all right?" he says. "Do you want me to pull over?"

"Where?" I say, still laughing. "Don't worry, I'm not sick. I
just—does she go by Pam? Do you call her Pam? My sister's
name is Carla, we call her Carly—" I pull myself up, hit the lever
to raise the seat and my eyes are beginning to tear, the sobriety
was a trick, *The damn trees,* I'm thinking—"she has a boyfriend
now and Jesus, she probably calls him Eddie—"

He's looking dead ahead, both hands on the wheel though the
road is straight, a deep slide in the dark. I roll my window down
and he glances at me.

"I thought you wanted to sleep."

I do. But I'm awake and I think I'll stay that way for the drive
at least, the way back in, no reason to waste such a beautiful
night—this is what you'd like to hear me say, isn't it? If I were
someone else I'd rest my hand on the back of your neck and lean
over to kiss your temple, settle back into my seat and wrap my
soft sweater around me, maybe turn the radio on low. If you
were someone else you'd have my pants unbuttoned by now, fin-
gers greedy and rough and tobacco-stained, your tie loose
around your neck, everything ready, zigzagging fast through traf-
fic. These people are here right now though you only know
about one of them.

"Martha? Are you sleeping?"

"You should meet my sister," I say.

He sighs. "I didn't know you had one."

We're at our exit. He signals and slows the car along the
curve. "I do. I have a sister. We don't really look alike," I say.
"Why are you signaling?"

"What?"

"There's no one else here. There's no cars. I can understand stopping at red lights, but Jesus, Wesley."

He drives on.

———

Nothing I remember is useful to me now, and maybe that's just as well —better to have no map at all than the wrong one, better that there's no trail to follow back.

"Can I stay?" Wesley says. "I can stay." Three words, only so many ways to rearrange without losing the sense of them. We're in my house, in our coats, our winter skins. This is the time of year I always loved best, slow gray days, sleep as easy at noon as midnight, and I feel cheated.

"I can stay," he says again. "I talked to her before I came to get you. I don't need to be back home tonight." His face is flushed, a little boy who's got around curfew, almost guilty. If I close my eyes I can make him that, a boy; strip the weight from his arms and legs until they're whip-thin, furious with wanting, *What were you before you were this*, I think, *before you were anyone's husband? What were you at twenty-four, what did you promise the girls, what lies did you tell, what did they believe?*

He moves to light a candle. "I want to sleep with you," he says. He doesn't look at me. "I just—that's all I want. Nothing else."

And I know this is not a lie. *But was it ever? Did you say these words to someone once and mean them just a little, only enough to forget them as soon as forgetting was allowed? Were you sweet no longer than you had to be? Was time a friend or an enemy, did you turn the clock to the wall?*

"If that's all you want you might as well go."

"What? Martha——"

I take my coat off and toss it on the couch. The candle burns vanilla. "I'm not angry," I say. "That's not the point. But I think we shouldn't pretend that this is what we do. I'm tired, Wesley."

"That we do what? What?" His voice is rising with that panicky edge I remember from years ago, from late drunken nights in bathrooms, on corners; the voice that registers the end of things before the heart has a chance. "Martha, I don't know what you're talking about."

You do. You know it before you're ready to, but I have all the time in the world.

It's early, just nine o'clock: time for me to be sliding into stockings and heels, painting my mouth the red that Carly can't wear—too fair for that, her face eggshell white until it warms to gold in August. Time for me to be wrapping a scarf around my neck and waiting in the vestibule for Edward's headlights to flash, time for me to put on a face I haven't worn in so long.

Wesley still has his overcoat on, dark green, all-weather, something I imagine his students would wear. But they're not his students, exactly, and at this moment I can't think of what he might know to teach them.

"We don't sleep together, Wesley. That's not what this is about. You sleep with someone else. I'm not that person. I don't want to be." We're standing not even a foot apart, but it would take me years to get to him, and maybe that's more time than I have right now, maybe that's enough to know.

"Jesus, Martha, you're not making any sense—I don't—" He stops, his words all used up, the silence in the room the same silence his wife must hear, and this is something else I need to know. A little past nine on a Friday night is as good a time as any to fix things.

"I made a mistake." *I made a mistake nine times over, and you know this.* "I'm not angry," I say again, "but I think we've run this through."

He says nothing, and his bulk shifts, settles into something that I haven't seen since the first time he came into the store, and I remember this, the vagueness of him, as though he hadn't yet caught up with his body—the opposite of me, always ready to leave my own behind.

He nods, his eyes on the candle flame. Pamela is in St. Louis. I've never been there—*here* is the only place I've been, and here is not working. But I am ruthless, I will remember none of this, I will burn him from my skin nine times over. That I could love him is impossible, that I could let him stay is something worse. *What did you fill in me*, I think, *what space I didn't know about? And how can I close it up?*

"I'm sorry," I say, and the words are bitter, choking. There's no undoing to things. I close my eyes and wait for the sound of the door.

SATURDAY MORNING I'M UP early, be-
fore the alarm goes off, but any pleasure I would normally take
from this is missing. I wake up remembering.

The house is in order, nothing but my coat still on the sofa,
and even though I know it's ridiculous I look out the front win-
dow—the street is silent, empty, and what made me expect any-
thing else? He's home, in a place I can't even picture, though
how could it be much different from here? The streets in this
town are all the same, neither narrow nor wide, the houses set
just far enough back to seem habitable. No place is farther than
five minutes from anywhere else.

I close the curtains and make coffee, turn the television on to
a news channel, and the house fills with well-modulated voices,

voices that could talk you through anything. But there's nothing for me to be talked through.

I put on clothes, jewelry, a face. It's sunny and still, a good day for people to be out. Before I leave I turn off the television and hang my coat, and when I open the door the room fills with light. It's like a dollhouse, this living room, small and square, not close to big enough for life.

———

By the time Melissa gets in at noon my nerves are humming. The store is empty, the last few customers just out, all of them carrying bags. No one can argue with me today—whatever I put in their hands they buy.

"How's it going?" she says. She squeezes behind me and tosses her bag and jacket into the back room. Her fine skin is pale, dull; her eyes are shadowed.

"You know that awful belt buckle? That thing with the lumps of coral? Sold it." I run a total on the register and drink from my coffee cup. Cold. "What happened to you?"

"Am I late?" she says, looking stricken.

"You look a little ragged. Have a bracelet," I say. I hand her a polishing cloth and inlaid cuff.

"Oh. Really? I put makeup on. Diggs had a party last night. His parents were in New Orleans. He's dead tomorrow night, guaranteed. That's when they get home," she says, and looks at me to make sure I've understood. She rubs at the bracelet, her fingernails bitten to the quicks, skeins of colored thread woven around her wrists.

"Diggs?"

"This guy. We used to go out. I make a point of not talking to him in school but everyone was there last night, so you know. I can't believe someone bought that. That thing was nasty."

"I sold it to a very lovely woman who was looking for a gift for her son's twenty-first birthday. He'll be able to keep his pants up now." She doesn't get the joke, if it's a joke at all. I don't know anymore. "So, Diggs. Did you talk last night?"

She shrugs. "Yeah. I don't know. It's weird—I mean, he's okay. He's waiting to hear about a football scholarship, so he's all into that, and there were these freshmen there, so . . . " She reaches down for her bag and fishes out a case overflowing with makeup, extracts a compact and frazzled brush for her cheeks. "I don't know. He still calls me sometimes and I talk to him then but it's different. You know sometimes how when there's no one else around it's different?" She puts the makeup on the counter and pinches at her cheeks. They're mottled now, blotchy and uneven.

"Melissa, here." I tear a fresh paper towel off the roll and hand it to her. "Go wipe your face. I'll do it for you."

"Yeah? Okay." She disappears into the back and I hear water running. "When I was a freshman I was too scared to go to the big parties," she calls. "But these girls, man, you should see them. They wear these clothes—my mother would *never* have let me." She comes out and her face is clean and damp. I hand her the tube of moisturizer I keep behind the counter.

"Put this on. Just a little." She eyes it. "You're probably dehydrated."

"I had a Coke before I came."

"That doesn't count."

She uses the moisturizer and I set to work on her face. Her bag is stuffed—lipsticks in cheap plastic tubes, glittery eye shadow, blue mascara. "You really don't need all this stuff, you know," I tell her. Her face is raised to mine. I work dabs of foundation under her eyes with my finger. "You should get rid of that sponge," I say. "It's filthy."

She lets me work. Her chin and cheeks are soft—the face she'll have eventually is still buried, all sleeping bones and hidden angles. "Okay. And don't tell me you need more—the more you put on, the more obvious it is you're trying to hide something." She doesn't argue. "Look," I say. "Here. Why don't you run across the street and get something to drink?" I give her a five-dollar bill from my purse. "Get a lemonade or something. And get me a large coffee, black. We've got some aspirin in the back, too."

She jogs across the street, waits for cars to pass. Noon on a Saturday morning—some Saturdays were *all* morning, I remember, in bed past two, curtains drawn, voices and music from the night before still singing against the bright sun, and Carly still young enough to want to climb in bed with me, pull the sheets into a tent and say *Tell me. Who was there? Did you get kissed?*

Melissa pushes the door open with her hip, two Styrofoam cups balanced in her hands. "There were some people there from last night. They all looked worse than me." She sets the cups and change on the counter and starts to polish another bracelet. "I like this one." She turns it in the light, a delicate cuff set with pale violet stones. "What is it?"

"Iolite."

"Pretty," she says. She rubs at the silver with the cloth.

"Try not to get polish on the stones. So," I say. I sit on the stepladder, pry the lid from the cup. "Who was over there?"

"Just people. They said someone started bowling the trash cans after I left. Diggs is still cleaning up."

"Huh. That's new."

"Not really." She finishes with the bracelet and slips it on, over the strands of dingy cotton. It fits snugly—even her wrists are soft, dimpled and fleshy. "It's a thing people do. You set the trash cans at the end of the driveway and roll cans of vegetables or something at them—the big ones, you know, like you get at Sam's or the restaurant supply place."

"Where'd you get those?" I nod at her wrists. She takes off the iolite cuff and sets it on a velvet tray.

"Diggs. We used to give each other stuff. They're ratty," she says, "but you're not supposed to cut them off. They wear through and then you make a wish on them. I was supposed to call him when they got ready to break so we could go someplace and make a wish together." She shrugs, and I can see how exhausted she is, a little girl with a thousand wishes yet and no idea which to use first. "They're pretty close," she says, fingering the strands. "It's been seven and a half months."

Close is good, I think, *close to anything, even the end of something— close means you're moving.* She leans against the counter and rubs at her eyes, smearing mascara beneath them. *But don't keep such close track of time—that's the only thing. It will wear you down, sure as stones in water.*

"It got quiet, huh?" she says. She moves out from behind the counter to the door, watches the street. "I guess everyone's at lunch or something. What did you do last night?"

"Took a drive," I say. Easy as that. "I went north for a while, up to some little town and back. Stopped for a few drinks at a restaurant and came home."

This is the truth. This is what happened. The rest is superfluous, already fading.

"What town?"

"You know, I didn't even notice. The place was Fagin's, though. Brick building."

"Fagin's—sometimes we have the prom there. The parents don't like it because they think it's too far." She turns suddenly, crosses her arms in front of her. "Are you lonely?" she says. "I never hear you talk about anyone. I mean, do you *know* anybody here?" She's impatient; one foot bounces behind the other. "Graduation is in less than five months." *Time*, I think, *Oh, Melissa. You could tell me the number of days.* "Then everyone leaves. The only places I've been are New Orleans and Pensacola. I applied to Florida State. That's Tallahassee. No one else did. Who do you *miss?*" she says to me. Her eyes are smudged blue, cheeks shining through the powder. "I mean, like last night, who did you wish was there?"

A woman on the sidewalk pauses at the front window, bends over to look at a necklace—I know the one, a tier of citrine drops, sun-colored. Her hair is short, curly; her sweater is a nubby wool. She straightens and moves on.

"I miss my sister," I say. *I would rather she were with me than someone else.* "I miss someone I used to see." *Say their names. Say them together—what could happen?*

"Yeah?" Melissa comes back to the counter and leans over the register. "A boyfriend?" she says, and it's clear to me that this possibility had never occurred to her—she knows I'm not married, and what else could there be?

"Not exactly. We saw each other sometimes, went out."

"Like on dates?"

"Dates," I say. "I don't know. Something like that. We met up with people."

"In bars? God, I wish I could go to bars. Some of my friends have fake IDs but there's nowhere to go here." She punches the NO SALE button and the register drawer pops out against my knees.

There's always someplace to go. You'll get to Tallahassee and at first it will seem like heaven and you will wonder how you lived before it, how you got through the small bright days in this town. You will think about this town and you will wonder how it goes on without you; you will think of the roads leading in that you are not on and they will seem as

insubstantial to you as spun cotton. And eventually, you will stop think-
ing of this place at all, even if you should find yourself back in it.

"So," she says. "What happened?"

"With what?" I push the drawer back in.

"The guy. The *man*," she says, and rolls her eyes. "I guess you call them men, right? Where is he?"

Almost one on a Saturday—if he's at home he's still in bed, in the dark room at the back of the second floor, quieter than my house on its wider street. He has a Mason jar of tepid water on the night table, blue sheets bunched at his ankles, the sole of one foot exposed and facing the ceiling, a comma-shaped island.

"I have no idea where he is," I say.

In Tallahassee, everyone will be someone you've never seen before. You will look at them like a starving girl and imagine the taste of their salty skin on your tongue. For the first few weeks you'll barely eat and your stomach will cramp with wanting, with a world of people who could fill you, split you wide open. The most difficult thing will be choosing, and even that will be easy once you realize that every choice is impermanent; a week or a month or a day until your hands grow tired of what they touch, or until what they touch takes itself away. But you will be ready for this. You will be nothing like me.

———

Seven o'clock and Louise and I are in my car, flying north on the same road as last night.

"Where are we going?" Louise says. We're a few miles out of town and the sky is pitch. She's got the visor down, putting lipstick on in the mirror light.

"Just for drinks," I say. "Out."

"Where?" She presses her lips together and flips the visor up. "Tell me," she says. "I hate surprises."

Mrs.Walters, I said when I got home from work, *can Louise come out to play?* and she laughed, shook a cigarette out of her pack, and I took it, lit it in their pink living room and said *God, these are awful.*

Take her, she said. *Have her home by one and don't get fresh with her. Do you girls need some money? Get your coat, Louise. Go on. Martha, there's a plate of cookies in the kitchen. Bring them in.*

I brought the cookies and smoked the cigarette and held the door while Louise kissed Nana good-bye.

"Not too far," I say. The tires thump over potholes. "A place called Fagin's."

"Fagin's?" Louise laughs. "Martha, that's where all the old people go!" The road is empty, her lips pink and garish and sweet-looking, like candy. "Not there. There's another place. It's on the same road, you just have to go a little farther. How'd you wind up at Fagin's anyway?"

"I have no idea," I say.

"We used to have our proms there. They'd close the place down and clear the tables out and put a dance floor down." We're at the exit and I pull off, make the turn at the light. "Just keep going past it. Cues is a few miles up."

"Cues?"

"They have pool tables," she says. "So they'd set up a long table at the back with food and stock the bar with sparkling apple juice. At Fagin's, I mean. But Toby would load the truck with beer and whiskey, and everybody'd be going in and out all night." She flips the visor down again and adjusts her hat. It's black felt tonight, small and neat.

"You look nice, Louise," I say, and she does.

"You think? I don't even know anymore. I hardly look in mirrors. We've got the pictures," she says, "all those portraits we got taken. I look at those. I forget sometimes."

"Forget what?"

"Up here. Just past the curve—right. Pull in."

It's a gravel square of parking lot, cars tucked under the pines. The building is small, aluminum-sided with a wooden addition that looks like a backless garage.

"There's a spot," Louise says, and I see it, an empty space between two pickups. "The college is up the road. Where Toby went. I haven't been here since I don't remember."

We get out of the car and gravel crunches white under us. My heels are unsteady, Louise a half-stride ahead of me, the moon slivering through the trees and the air asleep. She pulls the door open and I follow her in. Two steps up to plank floors and a rectangular bar in the center, pool tables to the right and left and beyond the main floor.

"Careful," Louise says, and motions down, and I see that the wood floor is staggered every few yards, a step up in one spot, two down in another. "I don't think it got built all at once."

We sit at the bar, a few empty stools on either side of us. "It's just beer," Louise says. She wedges her purse between her feet. "Or soda, I guess. Is beer okay?"

"It's fine."

"Two Bud Lites," she says to the bartender, who eyes her for a moment, then turns to the cooler. There are only a handful of women here, all with men, all in tight jeans and patterned sweaters. The men wear jeans and baseball caps and flannel shirts, sleeves rolled up, arms compact and muscled. They could be twenty or forty-five, and none of them looks at us.

The bartender sets the bottles down. "You want a tab?" he says, and Louise nods. She looks around the room and smiles. "It's funny," she says. "I said to come here and as soon as I did I thought it would make me sad, but it doesn't. It isn't. It's funny how things work out." She drinks and the beer foams up into the neck of the bottle.

A girl punches at the lap of the jukebox across the room. It's sunk a few feet lower than where we sit and all I can see are her shoulders moving, her hair falling over them. She spins and looks over one shoulder, raises an arm and beckons to the far corner of the room.

"So what did you forget?" I say. Louise waits, confused. "In the car. About the pictures—you said you had the pictures but you forgot anyway."

"Oh. Oh God," she says, lets her head tilt forward, her nose almost touching the bottle. "It's so silly. I can't believe I was even thinking it. It's been so long since I've been anywhere. We used to go out a lot, though—I bet as much as you did." She lifts the bottle to drink and it's almost empty. She's not wasting any time. "I was pretty," she says. She looks at me and smiles and there is no pride in her round face, no vanity at all. "I used to be pretty. The boys all thought so, and my mother used to give me no end of grief about it. We'd be in the car coming home from church and she'd start in on it, go the whole way home, and get my sisters in, too, about how it was a sin to think too much of yourself, and stupid besides. They'd all go on," she says, and shakes her head. "And the worst part," she says, "the absolute worst, is that my sisters are nothing to look at. My mother either." She finishes the beer and nods to the bartender, waves her fingers between us. My bottle is still over half-full and I get to work at it. "And I'm not saying this to be spiteful, it's just true—they're all as nice as you could want but my goodness, Martha, I just want to tell them a little lipstick couldn't hurt." The bartender sets two more bottles down and as she thanks him her smile widens into a grin and she's laughing.

"What?" he says, hands on hips, and she shakes her head, helpless. The bartender moves off and Louise takes my arm and squeezes. "It's funny when you think how it turned out," she says. "Years and years."

———

She drinks for the next two hours, one beer after the next until I see the bartender watching us from the other side of the bar and how long he's been watching I don't know. But Louise doesn't notice this. She keeps her head moving, her eyes wide and only a little unfocused, and talks steadily, softly, one story tumbling into the next and the refrain comes more often than she could know, *It's funny I'm not sad you'd think I would be but I'm not it's funny it's funny* and nothing, as far as I can see, is funny at all.

I wanted to be a cheerleader but my mother wouldn't let me so I sat behind the bleachers with Toby and his friends and I made sure I kissed all of them before I decided on him. I picked him. It was all up to me.

I listen. When she takes my arm I steady it against the bar and hold her weight, less than I would have thought. She's drunk her lipstick off and the hat has crept back on her forehead, ashy-pale wisps high over her brow. The bartender leans against the cooler and taps a cigarette against the pack, eyes lidded, harsh and lovely. In another place.

And I was so worried I'd get pregnant but nothing happened and after we got married I didn't worry anymore but nothing happened then either. She stands, catches her ankle on the stool but rights herself. *I'll just be a minute.* She collects her purse and makes her way across the room, slow, deliberate. She gauges every step and disappears behind a wooden door that slams behind her and the bartender is in front of me, cigarette burning.

"Do you want me to cut your friend off?" he says. "Might not be a bad idea."

I consider this, and what I think about is the house, the close pink living room and cluttered kitchen, Nana in her chair with her drink and ashtray and television, in the dark quiet with her husband and son.

"What about if you brought a glass of water? And maybe just slowed down the beer?" He looks at me. He can see that I have no business taking care of anyone. "I don't want to take her home yet."

"Slow down the beer?" he says. "What the hell are you talking about?"

"Don't bring it so fast. Make her ask a few times or something. Jesus, I don't know," I say, and as fast as that I could cut his smug pretty throat. "She never gets out. I just think it would be nice if she could stay for a while. She's not driving."

He shrugs. "Stay till closing then. Don't let her get out of hand. Does she have money?"

"I have money. And she's the least likely person in here to get out of hand."

"What about you?" he says. His smile is familiar to me, the curve of bottom lip and mocking eyes. "Any chance you'll get out of hand?"

"What do you think?" I say. "Really. Tell me, I'm interested. I'm interested in your powers of observation. You've been staring at us half the night, so impress me. Dazzle me," I say. "What do we look like to you?"

He leans in until he's close enough to whisper. "She looks like a real nice girl," he says, and his smile is nothing but ice, "and you look like something that got dragged a few miles into town and called it lucky."

———

We stay until closing. The bartender brings Louise beers as fast as she can drink them. He calls her *Sweetheart*. We stay until the pool tables are empty and the floors are bare and I take her purse for her and help her on with her coat, my keys in my hand, and we walk to the door like cripples. The bartender tosses bottles into recycling bins, the noise knifelike and bright, and Louise looks around the room like a drowning woman. He watches us with no expression at all, looking through Louise until she is close to invisible; eating me piece by piece until there is nothing left of either of us.

THIS IS HOW TO GO HOME.

Say *home,* say *when,* say *where.* Say these things like you mean them. Say the first like you'll be able to find it and the second like you want an answer. Say the third when you realize you don't believe the first exists. Count out loud in your bed— sheep, cigarettes, minutes, whatever you can think of in your small room, and if you can think of nothing, get out of bed and count the stars, the trees, the houses along the street. Don't lose your place. Box after box after box. Count the number of streetlights between you and the interstate—close your eyes, you can picture them, you can count them with fingers to spare.

———

I dream that Louise and I are still in the bar. She is wearing a red dress and when she takes her hat off dark gold curls spill out of it. They nearly reach the floor. *Do you like it?* she says. *I wrap it around the bedpost at night. It's too heavy to sleep on. I know the bartender here—he'll bring us whatever we want.* She lifts a hand and he's in front of us, a face I haven't seen in years, sky-blue eyes and honey skin. *Martha*, he says, *how long's it been?*

Since high school. Since the accident—April. What about April?

It's only February, he says.

That comes later, Louise says. *This is my husband. We have to hurry, Martha. Here.* She lines up plastic prescription bottles on the bar. *What was that drink you told me about? Fill her up, Toby.*

That's not his name. His name's Sticky. His name's Frank. He uncaps the bottles and pours into them, something clear that smells like roses. *No*, I say, *I'm driving. Please don't.*

You're not driving, you're just tired, Louise says. *If you put your hair up you'll feel better. Toby drives at night. His hair doesn't take up any room at all.*

He looks at me. *My boat's outside* he says. His fingers are blue as his eyes, and he wraps them in Louise's hair, tugs through the curls until handfuls begin to come out, gold ribbons falling over her dress, the stool, the floor, and the floor is water, shallow and still, a dark mirror. I lift my feet and see that they are bare.

Closing time, ladies, he says. *Time to swim.*

———

I open my eyes and flip the sheets back. My hand comes away wet from my chest, skin hardening into gooseflesh as the cool air hits. I pull on a robe and open the window, smell the rain that's still far enough away to be nothing but a breath.

My own breath is shallow, uneven. I remember waking in the middle of the night when I was a little girl and taking my pillow and blanket to the floor by my bed, curling up there and disappearing back into sleep. There was nothing to be afraid of.

I feel my way through the living room, trail my hand along the wall. The light on the answering machine blinks—once, twice, three times, four. His wife is in St. Louis. Yes.

Count the messages you'll erase before listening, the garnets in the first necklace you ever made, red as your mother's lipstick. Count all the husbands you know who aren't yours, count your kisses. Start with the first, and if you can't remember the first start with the last, and if the last has left your lips bitter erase it along with the messages.

Count the number of days the year has used up—do this by subtraction, by turning each day in upon itself, folding it small enough to fit in a calendar square, in a thimble, in a garnet bead. String them together, fasten them around your neck—they belong to you, these days, and when they become too heavy shut them in a drawer with the blessings you do not count.

I press a button on the answering machine and the tape whirrs backward.

Count the calls you didn't get, count the nights you watched your sister in the alley behind the house, her steps from the gate to the back door, a boy behind her waiting to make sure she got in safely before going back to the party they'd left, his night just beginning. Count the nights you stood in your doorway waiting for familiar headlights to slow and stop, for someone to speed you to a crowded bar where nothing was left to chance, the night choreographed by the two of you and danced once a week or twice at most, every move entire, every silence perfect and without surprise or blame. And if this struck you as tiresome then, if you imagined something better in a green small place you'd never seen, you have time to reconsider now.

Sleep is close as rain. Pull the blankets up, you're almost there.

Count the babies you don't have yet. Say *yet* like you said *home*—like you mean it, like the only thing between you and them is time. Unfold the days and smooth them out like the notes you hid in your binder at school, full of breathless secrets. *Write back soon*—you never did, you gave nothing, the safest thing. But count the babies now, make up for your mother, your sister, your neighbor; make no excuses for your vanity or cowardice. What stopped you? What was it that made your gut clench up at the thought of opening your legs for anything other than impermanence?

Tell yourself this: that it was right, that you knew your limits better than anyone could, that so far your heart has only opened enough for small things, wrong things; that you are still waiting and there is still time. Tell yourself that time is a gift, finite and constant, that turning the clocks to the wall stops nothing. Tell yourself this until you believe it.

You are not home, not yet. That comes later, if you're lucky. Count yourself lucky.

Spring COMES WITHOUT MY seeing. There is no last cold snap, no stray flakes of snow or heavy rain or lowering of sky. The sun does not shine any brighter than it did in October or January and the days grow warmer by two degrees or three, invariable, barely noticeable, so that there is no one day when I prop the front door open or push all the windows up; no morning when I wake to pale green on bare wet branches. The trees are the trees, dark and changeless.

My house is clean, my refrigerator stocked, my skin flawless. I dust and vacuum every weekend and cook every night, take leftovers to work with me in plastic containers. I do not fall into bed with makeup on. I floss. These are important things, I tell myself, and on some level I believe this. But to settle on the couch at nine o'clock and realize there is nothing left to do is a terrifying thing.

At the store I order gifts for the graduation season: tiny diplomas and mortarboards to string on necklaces or charm bracelets. They are cheap and light enough to crush under the heel of a hand. I order spring birthstones—synthetic pearls and emeralds, zircons—and arrange displays in the front windows with hand-lettered signs and dried flowers. Kerry and Melissa go through catalogs to choose their jewelry for the prom and I order enough to stock—colored rhinestones glued to flimsy alloy tiaras or wire cuffs that will turn a wrist green in an hour. These are the things I sell, and the rest of it, the Chinese turquoise with its spiderweb of veins, the deep red North African carnelian, gathers dust. I rearrange and polish, stack rings three high on my finger, drape necklaces over the women who come in and purr over their shoulders at their reflections in the mirror. They buy five-dollar charms and ask for gift boxes. They thank me and hurry out as though they have someplace to go, and I smile as though my life depends on it. Which, in a sense, it does.

————

When Wesley comes in I'm pulling rings from tiny Ziploc bags and sorting them by size. He has a leather book bag over his shoulder and two cups of coffee in a cardboard tray.

"Good morning," he says, and his voice surprises me in a way his physical presence does not—I've been ready to see him for weeks, in the car or at the grocery store, by chance, at random; ready to duck away, something I know how to do—but his voice is something different. I could close my eyes and hear it in the silence of my house, unavoidable.

"It's okay. I brought you some coffee." He eases the cups from the holder and sets them on the counter, careful not to disturb the piles of rings. "I can't stay long."

"Playing hooky?"

He smiles, rubs his cheek. "They're going nuts over there. The seniors—you'd think they were trying to get themselves expelled. Got one in my office every fifteen minutes. One of them rearranged all the books in the library. I think it was the first time he was actually in it."

I can see him with them, a wry smile, pencil bouncing between his fingers, patient, and I am ashamed.

"Martha," he says.

"We never did anything like that. I think we were unimaginative."

"I'm sorry," he says.

"Excuse me?"

"I came here to tell you I'm sorry." There's color in his face—he's been spending time outside.

"For what? I don't—"

"Listen to me. I was wrong. I put you in an awful position and I shouldn't have done that." He picks up a ring and turns it in his fingers, perches it on the tip of his pinky. It barely comes to the quick of the nail. "But it's been a long time since I've seen someone like you." He sets the ring down, careful not to let it bounce. His hand drifts over the piles of silver. The abstraction that I remember from the first time I saw him is back, wrapping him like a caul. The only thing clear about him is his voice, tempered, almost girlish. "You were beautiful, Martha. And you were someone new."

"Were?" I say. I try a smile.

"Are. But that's not the point. I thought you'd done this before."

"Done what?"

He doesn't look at me—hasn't really, in fact, since he came in. He's moving the rings, spiraling the piles out in a widening circle. It's all I can do not to snatch his hand away.

"I'm working on those," I say. His hand stills, hovers.

"How're you doing here? Business-wise, I mean."

"Well enough."

"I saw Kerry the other day. She's excited about the prom—got her date, the dress. Arguing with her mother about the curfew. She wanted me to call home for her."

"Wesley—"

"I thought you understood what would happen. It's a small town, Martha—I wasn't planning to do anything stupid."

"You're not making sense," I say. I sweep the rings toward me and begin re-sorting.

"If you would just *listen*," he says. "I never intended to leave my wife. No dramatics, Martha, not around here. Not with you." He's smiling, but underneath is something ugly.

That's not how things went, I think. *You begged me.*

Didn't you?

"As far as apologies go, this one ranks right up there," I say. His smile widens, lips almost colorless in the cast of his skin, eyes milky and vague.

"Girls like you." He shakes his head, runs a thumb under the shoulder strap of his bag and re-settles it. "What did you do before you came down here? Fuck some jackass for drinks and think it counted?" His voice is friendly, amused. "I grew up around girls like that. Don't really miss them—I just like to visit every once in a while." He picks up one of the coffee cups and sips. If I drank from the other I would leave a lipstick mark on the white plastic lid, something he has no right to see.

"The girls at school," he says, "they've got themselves all worked up, like the next few weeks are it, like after that there's nothing. They're desperate. You can smell it on them. You know who was the worst? Your neighbor. Louise." He laughs. "What, you think I didn't know her? We still talk about Louise. Every time you turned around she had her legs wrapped around that gearhead boyfriend. You have to feel sorry for her, though." He shrugs. "For all of them, I guess. Especially the pretty ones."

"I think we're finished here," I say. He's looking around, squinting at display cases against the glare of sun on glass. He has all the time in the world.

"You think?" He takes a long swallow and sets the cup down. "Yeah, I guess so." He steps back, pulls a pair of sunglasses from his jacket pocket. "I bet you had long hair, didn't you? You had long hair and you wore your skirts just a little too short, and a little too much makeup, maybe, and when you fucked them you acted like it was gold, and maybe they believed it, but as soon as they left they realized it was nothing. Because they could get it anywhere, and for a lot less trouble. That sound about right?" he says pleasantly. "Okay. I'm running late. God-damn. Listen," he says. He's at the door, holding it open with a shoulder, and the breeze that comes in is warm and sweet. "If I see you anywhere I'm going to come over and say hello. And if my wife's with me I'll introduce you. And trust me—she won't think anything. She'll take one look at you and you'll be a good joke for weeks."

———

In school, the young nuns were the ones we wanted. Some were just a few years out of college, eager and sweet; others, slightly older, had traveled, done missionary work. They decorated their classrooms with souvenirs they'd brought back from Mexico or India or North Africa—ornate masks, musical instruments, leather-bound books in languages we could not read. They had short hair and smooth skin and wore denim wraparound skirts or raw cotton blouses, the large wooden crosses sometimes hidden under collars embroidered with vines and flowers. A few were going to night school for degrees in social work, and they read their own textbooks during study halls, tapping fat yellow markers against white teeth.

The older ones were different, most still in full habit, only a sliver of forehead showing under the wimple, thick stockings and tan lace-up shoes at the other end. They had taught our parents before they taught us and sometimes called us by our mother's or father's name, and we learned not to correct them. They led us in prayers at the beginning and end of each day, and while the younger sisters prayed for an end to nuclear weapons or famine or political oppression (not only in parts of the world we'd never seen but *in our own back yards* they made sure to tell us), the older ones drilled us with decades of the Rosary and protracted Acts of Contrition. We bowed our heads and closed our eyes and tried to stay awake.

But Sister Mary Paul was an exception. Nearly seventy, solid and arthritic with grossly swollen ankles, she was kind, patient; when one of us gave a wrong answer she could correct us without malice and we were not embarrassed or bitter. If she called us by our parents' names, which she did only rarely, she was quick to apologize and laugh at her own forgetfulness. In the twelfth grade we had her last period for history. At the beginning of the year she handed out mimeographs of the curriculum through Christmas, but Fridays were left blank. She would only smile and say nothing when we asked her why.

That first Friday of the school year we were too tired to be excited by the end of the week. It was hot, a sticky Baltimore September that was no different from July or August. The classroom windows were open and the smells of chalk and sweat were faint, mixed with hot asphalt and cooking from the houses across the street. We had barely settled into our seats when Sister Mary Paul moved to the front of her desk and spread her arms.

"Move the desks," she said. "Over to the sides—like that. Good. Leave an aisle down the middle." We cleared them, toed our stacks of books in messy piles by the radiators.

"Girls over here," she said, pointing at the bank of windows, "and boys there, by the blackboard." We bumped each other, slid past warm bodies and leaned up against the wall and windows. On another day we would have been noisy, keyed up; on that day the loudest sound was our shoes on the freshly waxed floor.

"Sister Helen used to play this game with you in the third grade—do you remember?" Sister Mary Paul had taken a stack of index cards and two push-bells from her desk; she put the bells on the edge of it, side by side, and shuffled the cards, her smile a clear sky. "You're all going to line up single file, two rows straight back. The two of you at the front will listen to a question I read"—she waved the cards over her head—"and ring the bell if you know the answer. Whoever gets the answer first goes to the back of the line for another turn, and whoever gets it wrong sits down. Are you ready? Come on then, line up."

I remembered the game—we'd played it with arithmetic flash cards and Sister Helen had posterboard charts tacked to the bulletin boards with stars next to the names of those who won most often. She'd divided the classroom in half and called us the red team and the blue team.

"God, I can't take this today," Connie moaned in my ear. We were at the back of the line. She leaned her head on my shoulder. "I'm tired. I'm cranky. I'm not in the mood for this. If I wanted to be on a game show I'd call Wink Martindale."

What is the capital of Sweden?

Where was the Declaration of Independence written?

What year did the Boer War begin?

Who killed Archduke Franz Ferdinand?

We shuffled to the front of the room. It was after two o'clock, the time of day when we put our heads on our books and took notes we couldn't read, facing the clock. The bell dinged. I wasn't listening to the answers. I was watching the sides of the room, the blackboard side empty, the other slowly filling. One girl, two, five.

What is the major export of Brazil?

Which was the first state to secede from the Union?

Ding, ding, ding.

At the front, I stood next to Andy Callas. He was a head taller than I was, thin and awkward and slow, more than a little mean. He leaned slightly forward, the heel of his back foot off the floor, one hand poised at his hip. Sister Mary Paul thumbed the cards, smiling.

"God, Andy. It's just a game," I said under my breath. His body was humming.

In what year did Albert Einstein win the Nobel Prize?

Ding.

"1921," I said.

Sister Mary Paul nodded. "Very good, Martha," she said. Andy looked at me, his face crimson.

By the end of the period there were four girls left in the line. We slid behind one another after each turn, necks damp and collars limp, turn after turn against the fifteen boys who snaked in their line next to us.

"A little incentive," Sister Mary Paul said, rubber-banding the cards and picking up a notebook and pen. "I'll be keeping track of the results, and there will be a prize for the winning team at Christmas. Girls," she said, turning to the windows, to the shiny faces and wrinkled skirts, "you'll have to do better. I know that history isn't your best subject, but you should at least try."

The boys laughed, high-fived one another. We moved the desks back into rows, collected our books and stood for the prayer—*O my God, at the end of this day I thank You most heartily for all the graces I have received from You*—and I watched Sister Mary Paul, her eyes closed, hands folded tight under the cross around her neck; the girls lifting the hair from the backs of their necks, tilting their faces to the ceiling; and the boys, even in the heat and quiet some part of them moving, a bouncing leg or nodding head, and thought *What graces?*

————

I lift Wesley's cup to throw it out. There's a smear of coffee on the glass under it and I wipe it with the sleeve of my shirt. Laundry the day after tomorrow. My own coffee is barely warm, bitter; the mark of my lips red and neat on the cup. I look through the drawer for a packet of sugar beneath the pencils and price tags, and I concentrate, try to remember his face in my living room, eyes wide and confused and almost panicked—*Isn't this the way it happened?*—but what I remember instead is the sticky hot classroom like the ones Melissa and Kerry are in now, the same still air, the same recklessness, and the same boys, tall and vain and fearless. They are desperate for nothing; there is not a thing in this world that they could use up.

"**W**HY DON'T YOU JUST FLY?" my mother says. "Put the ticket on my credit card. Joseph, tell her."

"It would be easier, sweetheart." He's on the extension. As long as they're not both talking at once I'm fine. I'm in the living room, front door open, and the breeze coming in is almost too warm already, but it's air, and it's moving.

"Really, Martha," she says. "There's just no reason for you to drive all that way when you don't have to. You can have our car when you're here. And that way you'll be able to stay longer."

"I can't stay that long one way or the other. I can't leave the store closed that long," I tell her. Across the street a woman with gloves on is kneeling by a strip of mulch in front of her house. One of my neighbors. She's careful to keep her back to the street, to my open door.

"I don't want to have to worry about you driving. It's such a long way—"

"Two days of easy driving, Mom, I've done it before. It's not a big deal, really." But it is a big deal, it's two days with the windows open and the radio on, going fast, cups of bad coffee shot with flavored creamer and too much sugar hooked to the door, and at the end of the first day, one sweet night in a hotel that could be anywhere. Something metallic flashes in the sunlight—a spade. The woman across the street is digging. She could look over if she wanted; my living room is spotless. There's a bottle of wine on my coffee table, unopened. It's ten-thirty; I'm waiting till noon.

"So what's going on down there?" my father says. For him, the subject of the drive is over.

"Not too much, Daddy. Cleaning the house today. I might go out later."

"Good girl. Okay, I'm hanging up," he says, as much to my mother as to me.

"Where?" she says, when the extension clicks down.

"Where what?"

"You said you were going out."

"I said I might. I don't know yet." It's force of habit, I think, this mother-talk. Even with her children grown she keeps on; there is no other way to speak to us.

"Well. Your sister will be happy to see you."

"What's she up to? We haven't talked for a while." The woman across the street rises on one knee, plants the spade and leans in before moving the other leg to stand. "She was seeing someone, wasn't she?"

"Edward," my mother says. "A little older than her, but nice enough. Your father liked him."

Did he? Edward must have loved that, to come into that house and talk to the two of you about business, about real estate, the things I

*didn't listen to, didn't hear; to talk to you like that while Carly looked
on. Did he drink a glass of wine? Did he look at the pictures? Did he
look too long?*

"I don't know what's going on with them now, really. They
were seeing a lot of each other—she said he was driving up to
see her at school, but I can't imagine what he'd want to be doing
up there. I'll tell you," she says, and for a moment the terrain
shifts and I am her confidante. "I think she was coming down
here. Just sneaking in, not saying a word. Staying at his place."
She waits for me to respond to this. Anything I have to say she
would not want to hear.

"So she'll be there when I'm home?" My neighbor is moving a
flat of yellow flowers down from her porch, slow on the steps,
testing the hold of one foot before moving the other. No one
else is out.

"Oh sure. She'll be done with school by then. And we won't
have to argue to get her home. And it worries me, I'll tell you—
it's not that there's anything wrong with him, we only met him
that once, but she just seems so—or—" she is getting frus-
trated, standing by the sink, rubbing at a stain on the drain board
with her thumb. I know this. My mother's words dry up, the
closer they get to the bone. The stain on the drain board is
something she can manage.

She used to be lovely, my mother. Carly's mother was different.

"She's a big girl," I say. "Too damn old to still be in college."

"She graduates in August. And she's just fine where she is. She's
not like you, Martha."

You should get Edward's opinion on that.

"So how much older is he?" I say. I should be careful, I should
stop this.

"Your age, I imagine. I don't know, Martha, I hardly saw him."

"My age." *Careful*, I think, *don't correct her, don't slip.*

"Well. Maybe you could talk to her when you're here. Just see what she has to say. Would you do that?"

"Yeah." Talk to her—how? It's a foreign language to us, the way sisters talk. We don't know it well enough to sustain a conversation. Gestures, monosyllabic utterances, meaningless questions; two strangers in a new country. "Mom, I have to go. I have stuff to do."

"At least think about the ticket," she says. "It doesn't make sense for you to drive all this way. Just let us know. I don't need to be worrying about both of you. And call your sister. See if you—well, see what she says."

I promise to do this and when we hang up my mother is pacified, happy enough to start tonight's dinner. It's eleven A.M. I take the bottle of wine into the kitchen—out of sight, out of mind—and pour the last of the coffee to drink on the porch. My neighbor is kneeling again, her profile to me this time, setting the flowers into the holes she's been digging. When she reaches for a plant she turns enough to see me sitting here and I wave, cup to my lips, a barefoot woman in jeans enjoying the morning. She wraps both hands around the cardboard pot and ducks her head to the earth.

———

This is a house where someone lives. I don't know how it happened, but everything here has a look of permanence; unfamiliar to me, foreign. They are things that I've taken with me from place to place—the worn chairs from the corner of my parents' living room, the couch I bought when I moved in with Connie, but I can't picture them in these other rooms. It is as though they have always been here. I must have done this myself, anchored them so, but I have no memory of it. I remember telling the movers where to put things, standing aside and pointing, saying *Don't worry, it's fine there,* and after they left pushing at a corner of a table with my foot just enough to feel as though I'd had a hand in putting it there. The furniture sits where it was dropped that first Monday and has somehow grown into the floors. I couldn't move it if I tried. The candle dishes, the stack of magazines—if I flipped to the bottom one I would not be surprised to see it had been delivered here twenty years ago.

I have never seen pictures of my mother's first house, the one where she stayed with her first husband. I don't even know where it is, though it can't have been far from where she—I—grew up. Nothing is. I have been here six months, as long as she lived with him, and I wonder if she looked around their house and saw the rest of her life, potlucks in the kitchen and Christmas parties by the front window, bowls of punch and canapés, children on the sofa. I wonder if she saw Carly and me then, or if those children were different, more of a different father and less of her in their faces. I don't even know his name.

I wonder if she saw these things and believed them, or if, instead, she knew, my mother with her shiny flip of hair and narrow skirts; if she looked around that house and saw time sliding away already, if she saw what was waiting for her.

The pots and pans are arranged in cabinets, lids stacked and balanced alongside. There is a drawer for dish towels, extra sponges sealed in cellophane; spices lined up over the stove. Who did this, who took the time? When I lived with Connie our apartment was a riot of clothes and cloudy glasses. She was not there enough to notice; her overnight bag on her shoulder and keys in her hand on her way to Don's house, *I'll see you tomorrow afternoon*, before the door slammed shut behind her, and I learned myself to look past it all. *This is where I live now*, I told myself, *this is where people will come to see me*. But when I packed my things a few years later I had no illusions that I would not be packing them again.

A closet for cleaning supplies, vacuum cleaner tucked in the corner, thin phone books stacked on the shelf, their edges true. The freezer stocked and ice tray full, a grocery list on the refrigerator door, winter clothes in the back closet. Whoever lives here takes great care. Whoever lives here means to stay.

———

At dusk I walk next door to ask if Louise will watch the house while I'm gone. I haven't seen her since the night I took her out, and I haven't heard her singing in the morning. I thought to check on her the day after I brought her back, but I didn't want to force her to tell me that everything was fine.

The door opens before I can knock. "I'm sorry," Louise says. "I didn't mean to scare you. But I was up here and I saw you walking over. I was going to check the mail." There are shadows beneath her eyes and she smells faintly of vinegar. Her hair is wrapped in a flowered scarf. It's the first time I've seen her that she hasn't been smiling. "Do you want to come in?"

"It's nice out," I say. She glances behind her and shuts the door. We sit on the step, look out over the empty street. "So how are you? What's been going on?"

"Oh, not too much. Nothing, really." She wipes her hands along her pants. "I wanted to come over, but . . . I'm sorry, Martha. I didn't mean to be such a bother that night. And I feel so stupid—"

"Stop," I say. "You weren't a bother. We went out and had fun, right?"

"Is that what it was? I guess I forgot." Her laughter is thin, bitter, and though I've never heard anything like it from her it makes sense. She has every reason to sound this way. "I meant to come over and apologize, but I don't even remember coming home. And the next morning I felt so bad, and Nana thought it was so funny." She shakes her head. "Nothing's going on. I'm volunteering up at the church for the clothes drive. One of my sisters asked me to. They need help sorting."

"Well, I had a good time," I say. "I hadn't been out in forever. It was nice."

"What about that car?" Louise says. She doesn't look at me. "The one I used to see in your driveway." She's working at the hem of her pants, pinching it between two fingers, and I have the sense that she's been saving this, waiting for me to do something as insulting as lie to her. I dragged her out of my car and left her at her door because I was tired of her, because I was finished with her. "Brown car," she says. "I bet you went out with him. I bet that was *nice*." She spits the word out as though it's poison. "Sometimes I'd see him drive by when you were home but he wouldn't stop. Did you know that? Just went up and down the street a few times. Mrs. Myers across the street saw it, too. She'd watch out the front window. I thought she was going to call the cops or something. I bet you had fun with him. I didn't see who it was," she says, "but the thing is, it would've been real easy for me to find out. And I'm thinking you didn't want anyone to find out, right?" She looks at me in the fading light. "Don't make things up," she says, and the anger is gone from her voice. "I'm not stupid. Just because I live the way I do doesn't make me stupid."

"I know that," I say, and I know, too, that this is not even close to enough. The streetlight at the end of the block glows, faint and white, a star that doesn't move. The breeze is up and my hair is moving, long enough now to brush my shoulders. "I know you're not, Louise. I'm sorry. I wish there were something else I could say." But of course there is. There is no end to things—I could say my sister is happy and I could tell her how she came to be this way. I could say I came here because I wanted this quiet and these trees and the broken sky above them, because I thought the sun would burn me clean of all the useless things I know: how to lie back, legs open and eyes closed, heart somewhere in between; how to speak around the truth and wait to be believed—I could make a lie out of making a bed. I could tell her this.

She sighs, reaches over and catches my hand in both of hers. They're large, the skin of her palms thick, grainy. "They were all looking at you, that night in Cues. I could tell when I got up to go to the bathroom, they were all turning around to see if you were still sitting there. And I thought for sure when I came back you'd be with someone, he would've gone over and I was even thinking maybe he'd have a friend, just someone to talk to. For me, I mean." There's a burst of noise behind us, screeching tires and gunshots, then applause and laughter. Nana in her chair, the television flickering. "Then I came out and you were still by yourself. And I bet you didn't even notice."

"That I was alone? Louise—"

She releases my hand and shakes her head. "That's not how I mean. I mean, I bet you weren't worried about it, you weren't even *thinking* about it. Because how often do you sit alone? When you're out someplace? I *remember*," she says, still shaking her head, stubborn, an impatient little girl. "I remember what that was like, not worrying about being by yourself because you knew it wouldn't last." She flips the ends of the scarf behind her and stands. "I should go in. I've got dishes left, and laundry, clothes to sort . . . maybe we could do something again," she says. "Not go out. But maybe I could come over one night when you're not busy."

Busy. I think of my house, waiting. The flowers in the yard across the street are small pale flags in the dark. Louise's hand is on the doorknob, the cluttered pink room on the other side, the television, Nana, tiny soaps in crystal dishes, singed pot holders on the table, closets spilling over with clothes and ghosts tangled in them.

"We can do that," I say. I stand. My feet are bare, they've been bare all day. I feel weightless. Louise ducks inside, and it occurs to me that I've forgotten to ask what I came here for. My house doesn't need watching, or whose-ever house it is. Regret is too small a word to fill what is empty there.

THE DRIVE UNWINDS LIKE a ribbon. Flat land begins to breathe, exhalations rising up on either side of the road, first small hills then steeper higher ones, and the trees become smaller and wider in response, a pale deciduous green, and everywhere mild blue sky, the season taking hold. Too early yet for vacationers packed into cars, pillows and Kleenex boxes obscuring their windows.

My house is shut tight—bed made, counters clean, every cushion smooth, floors swept and curtains drawn. I put a hold on the mail and leave a note tucked in Louise's box. *Dear Louise, I'm so sorry. I have to leave town for a few weeks—family business. Please keep an eye on the house for me. I'll call as soon as I get back. Martha.* And at the bottom my parents' phone number. *Call if you need anything.* Pointless—what could she need that I could possibly give her? This is something I try not to think about.

Wytheville, Virginia, at dusk: the top of the exit empties straight into a strip of gas stations, convenience stores, motels. *Inns*—Rodeway, Ramada or Comfort; Econo if you're in the mood for a *lodge,* and from any parking lot I-81 is visible, winding like a black river below. Wytheville backs up to the interstate; two-lanes run parallel and above it and prefab houses face each other across the span of it. Every town along this stretch is like this, so that anyone could sit on their front porch and watch the semis fly past below.

I pull into the first lot on the right, get out of the car and stretch. It's an easy fifteen degrees cooler than when I left the house and the skin on my belly marbles up, contracts, but the sky is a fine soft gray, unbroken across the hills. I pull my overnight bag from the backseat and lock the car.

The lobby is bigger than I expected, low-ceilinged, a sunken area in the center with chairs and sofas, lamps on dark wood end tables, and beyond this the entrance to what looks like a bar. I stand at the counter and wait for the man behind it to drink from his soda and wipe his mouth with a cloth napkin.

"I need a single room, inside access if you have it."

He leans toward me and points to a hallway behind him. "Only first floor," he says.

"That's fine." I take my wallet from my bag and he punches some keys, peers at the computer monitor.

"Twin beds?"

"One double, if you have it." The parking lot was three-quarters empty. He punches more keys and exhales, squints at the screen.

"Room 118. Queen-size bed, eighty dollars a night. How many nights?"

"Just one." I slide my credit card across the counter—I won't know the name of this place until I get the bill. He processes the card and hands it back to me with a heavy plastic passkey in an envelope.

"Checkout's at noon. Straight back on the right."

"Do they serve dinner?" I motion to the bar.

"There's a menu in the room. Bar serves till eight." He steps away from the counter and picks up his glass. "Enjoy your stay."

"I will certainly do that," I say. "Thank you." I collect my things. He's already sitting, a pencil stub in his hand and a crossword book folded open on his lap.

The hall is narrow; it smells of carpet cleaner and faintly, under that, of bleach. When I get to my room I feed the key into the slot, push the door open when the green light blinks. It's a hotel room like thousands of others, perfect, the bleach smell stronger at the bathroom door, bland recirculated air throughout. I set my bag on the bed and adjust the temperature gauge on the radiator, turn on the TV and go into the bathroom. Plastic shower curtain and shower cap, plastic cups in plastic sleeves, little plastic bottles of shampoo and conditioner. I unwrap the soap and wash my hands, take one of the cups back to the bed with me.

In my bag is a change of clothes, makeup case and address book, a bottle of wine and a corkscrew wrapped in clean underwear. I open the bottle and pour a cup, look over the laminated menu propped on the night table. Burgers, chicken strips, nachos and sandwiches, and I toss the menu to the floor. I flip the channels, looking for local news, but there is none, there is only the cable news that I could be watching in Texas or New York or any place in between; in London or Tokyo, if I had ever been to places like that. The radiator hums.

I can imagine grand hotels, doormen in waistcoats and gloves opening taxi doors, polished brass handrails and vases of flowers at the desk, in the rooms; thick leather-bound books of services offered and white robes laid across the bed, windows that look out onto Central Park or the Via Veneto or the Champs Elysées, but I cannot imagine anything better than this small box with its parking lot and exit ramp and interstate, nothing beyond the windows but asphalt and grass and empty sky, nothing to indicate where you are or how you got here.

I strip and turn the shower on, wash my hair and then my body with the shampoo and use two towels to dry off. There's nothing for me to put on but the clothes I brought for tomorrow—everything else is packed in the trunk of the car—and so I wrap myself in a damp towel and turn the bedspread down. The sheets are soft and thin, almost translucent from washing.

There is the bottle of wine and cup, the address book at the foot of the bed, and in my bag a pack of cigarettes I bought at a gas station in Tennessee. It's eight o'clock—everyone I might want to call is finished with dinner, still awake, ready to answer their phones should they ring, to take a call from Paris or Tokyo or Wytheville, Virginia, *It's so lovely here, it's just what I hoped it would be only better, wish you could see it!*

I unwrap myself from the towel and toss it to the floor, pour another cup of wine and light the first cigarette. I don't need the address book, I know the number by heart.

Reid picks up the phone and I ask for Edward. He hesitates. I don't say hello and for a minute I think he'll ask who it is, but he doesn't. If he knows my voice he gives no indication, and when he says he'll get Edward the line goes silent for too long, as though he's holding his hand over the mouthpiece.

"Hello?" His voice. He knows.

"I'm in a hotel in Berlin. It's the middle of the night here." Silence. "I'm in Australia. It's already tomorrow."

"Who is this?"

"You know," I say. "I'm sorry. I know I'm a little late." I splash more wine into the cup and mute the TV. My heart is somewhere in Alabama. I wait.

"Why are you calling now?"

"Because I'll be there tomorrow. Because my bet is that there's going to be some welcome-home dinner and you'll be there. You already know this, Edward. Is Carly there?"

"No," he says. He exhales. "There's no one here. I worked late today."

"How was work?"

"Fuck this, Martha. I don't—"

"I'm in a hotel room in Virginia. I drove most of the day and I stopped here and I missed dinner. The bar's closed. I have a bottle of wine and a bunch of wet towels in here with me." Water is trickling down my back and I pull the sheet around, try to get the damp hair away from my skin. The address book slides to the floor. "Please," I say. "Just a few minutes. Can you give me that? Can you talk to me for just a little while? Because I don't think—I'm not staying long. In Baltimore, I mean."

"That's not what your sister said. She's excited. She thinks you'll be here for a few weeks. Did you do anything to disabuse her of that notion?"

"I haven't talked to her."

"I know that," he says, and my flesh opens for this small knife. In the mirror my face is a pale disk, my chest and arms and stomach whiter than that. "You'd be surprised at what I know."

I look around the room and imagine a wheeled table covered with cream linen, a bud vase, champagne flutes and silver domes over the plates. The bottle of wine is half-empty. I light another cigarette off the end of the last.

"Do you know about Nick?" I say. "Nick was a boy I knew when I was Carly's age, a little younger. I thought we'd get married. I didn't know any better then. Did she tell you about him? She thought he was gorgeous."

"Why are you telling me this?"

"Did you know I told her what to wear on your first date? You took her to Sotto Sopra and I told her to buy something new and fix her hair. I told her to look pretty for you."

"Are you drunk?" he says.

"I'm trying." I crush the cigarette out and it breaks, spills tobacco over the blanket. "I made a mistake. But I made it before I met you. Does that make a difference? All things being equal?"

"What things?" he says. "What *things*, Martha? You left. End of story."

"It's *not*—it wasn't you I was leaving. I'm trying to explain myself and it's pointless if you think you have everything figured out."

"Jesus Christ. Come on, Martha. Stop crying. Let's at least pretend to be adults here."

I touch my hand to my face and it comes away wet, and the part of me that cares is too far to reach. "I'm not trying to get you to change your mind."

"About what?" he says. His voice is rising, and I press the receiver tight against my face. I would swallow it if I could. "There's not a fucking thing for me to change my mind about. What do you want me to say to you?"

"Nothing." My voice is thick, disobedient. "Would it make a difference if I were somewhere else?"

"What? What are you talking about?"

"If I were somewhere else, if I went someplace for a better reason—I didn't do what I was supposed to do up there, I fucked up, it had nothing to do with you, I'm in this hotel room and I'm halfway there and I can't turn around because it wouldn't make anything better—"

"Martha." His voice is quiet now, too even, the voice you use to talk to a drunk. I can hear this. Everything is falling away in pieces. "I'm tired. You have to drive tomorrow. You should go to sleep."

"Listen to me," I say. "Just now. I'm trying—I won't keep you. I never said anything to Carly. I won't. But I thought things would be different. I thought a lot of things, and then I met you and I got confused because nothing was working the way it was supposed to."

"I never asked you for anything."

"I know that. I know. But if you had said to me, 'Let's go, let's leave, come on,' I would have. I would've gone with you, as long as it was someplace. Does that make a difference to you?"

I can hear him breathing. "Your parents miss you," he finally says, and I close my eyes.

"My mother was divorced for ten years when she was my age. Did Carly tell you that?"

"Martha—"

"It doesn't matter," I say. When I open my eyes the room takes its time swimming back into focus. "When I see you I'll shake your hand and say how nice it is to meet you. They've got cable here. I guess they've got it everywhere." He says nothing and I wait. I pour more wine and concentrate on breathing, shift my gaze carefully from TV to chair to night table. The ashtray is glass with fluted edges. If there's a logo on the bottom I can't see it. I'm in Wytheville, Virginia, and that's all I know.

"This is the longest phone conversation we've ever had," he says, and I squeeze my eyes closed but it doesn't matter, the tears are already on my lips. I wait for the next thing. "I had every intention of telling her."

"Don't." Simple words, safe; words I can get my mouth around. "You couldn't explain it. Do you look different?" I say. "I mean, when I see you—will I be surprised?"

"I don't think so."

"Okay. Then I'll be making the salad or something when you get there. I'll be busy. I'll say how nice it is to meet you and then we'll all drink wine and have dinner and sit around. You motherfucker," I say, and I start to gasp, great ripping breaths that are almost laughter. "You know her better than I do, there's no excuse, you should know—she's nothing like me, you pimp."

I can hear the trucks, the engines keening on the grade, the downshifts. They eat the silence on the other end of the line.

———

In the morning I lie still, eyes closed, and listen to the newscaster. Her voice is low and modulated, cities drop from her tongue like unstrung beads: Jerusalem, Belfast, Madrid. I think of the hotels, the people in them, and picture men in elegant suits with leather briefcases and tasseled loafers sitting in conference rooms, pitchers of water on long polished tables; women with dark lipstick and half-moon glasses, their hair twisted into elaborate whorls, legs silky and crossed. Their pens scratch at notepads; their feet swing back and forth. When the meeting is over they will stow their belongings into smart glossy satchels and click through the lobby, into the café, where they will sit in twos and threes and order bottles of wine, light cigarettes and lean back in their chairs, glasses off, eyes dark and aloof. They will drink their wine, eat from plates of cheese and fruit, tear off hunks of bread and brush the crumbs from their laps, their eyes never resting, and the waiters will watch them from the corner of the room, ready to leap to attention at the slightest gesture, as though fire might tongue from their fingertips.

I get out of bed and dress in clean clothes, repack my bag and check the room: empty wine bottle and full ashtray, the bedclothes kicked to a knot on the floor. I collect the towels and hang them over the shower rod, toss the used cups in the wastebasket and empty the ashtray on top of them. There are women in Jerusalem and Belfast and Madrid who did these same things while I was sleeping. I tell myself this. I am going home.

I COME DOWNSTAIRS DAMP from a shower and my mother has set the table already, place mats and silverware rolled in paper napkins. Five places. It's late afternoon, and the sun is warm through the propped-open back door.

"I would've done that," I say.

She's laying chicken pieces in a baking dish. "You drove all day. All *two* days," she says, and slides the dish into the oven. She was the only one home when I got in, Carly out shopping and my father playing cards at the lodge. We're still the only ones in the house, and for a moment I feel fifteen, ready to blow-dry my hair and put makeup on, bang out the door before dinner to meet Connie at the Exxon. "You look tired."

The headache I had this morning is almost gone. A glass of wine will finish it off. "I didn't sleep much last night. When's everyone getting home?"

"Dinner's at seven." She rinses her hands and sets the timer on the stove. "Connie and Don were at church with his parents this past weekend. I told them you'd be here. She said she couldn't remember the last time she spoke to you."

"Phone works both ways."

"That's not what I meant," she says.

She's wearing loose pants and a tunic with variegated stripes. "You look nice," I say. Her hair is chocolaty brown, freshly colored. "Is this a formal dinner? No one told me."

"Your sister's excited for you to meet Edward." She takes wine glasses from the cabinet and sets them on the counter, uncorks a bottle of red. Her voice is bland but her back is to me and this is deliberate, I think. She knows enough to let this statement hang in the warm air long enough for me to take hold of it, even if she doesn't know why. She's my mother. "Anyway. You should call Connie. She said they've done a lot to the house since you saw it." She brings the bottle and two glasses to the table and sits down. If the two of us have ever drunk wine alone together, I can't remember it. She's wearing lipstick and powder, but there are glimmers of sweat along her hairline.

I rub my face. "I should put myself together."

"Why bother? You're fine."

"Remember when you used to do my face for me?" I pour the wine myself. There's a bottle of arthritis-strength Excedrin by the sink. "You had that powder that smelled like old flowers. You made me look like a flapper."

"A little red lipstick never hurt anyone." She drinks and we sit, the smell of garlic and rosemary filling the room. It was what we had every Sunday, pasta and baked chicken, the funny pages spread on the family room floor and our book bags set against the back door, homework checked, tests signed, pencils sharpened and zipped in vinyl cases, and for a minute all this is so close I can barely breathe.

"I didn't tell you about my neighbor."

She nods. "Louise. You told me."

"No. That's not what I mean. She doesn't have any hair. She's twenty-two and she's bald. Her husband was killed in a car crash and she pulled all her hair out."

"That's terrible," she says, but her face closes off and she stands, goes to the stove and stirs the sauce with a wooden spoon. My mother is not unkind, or unfeeling, but she has made her life a safe place, and to entertain someone else's misery is to court it for herself. She taps the spoon against the edge of the pot and sets it on a saucer.

"She's twenty-two," I say again.

"I said it's terrible. What else do you want me to say? If you *told* me these things . . . "

I finish the wine and pour another glass to take upstairs with me. "I should get ready."

"You have time. I wanted to ask you—did you talk to Carly?"

On my bed upstairs is a pair of black pants and a silk top; heels still in my bag. *A little red lipstick never hurt anyone*—I'm meeting my sister's first real boyfriend; I don't want to look shabby. Anyone would believe this.

"I don't know any more than you," I say. "We don't *talk*, Mom—how could you have missed that? I'm not trying to make a point. I just—I was thinking about this on the drive up. I was thinking about Louise and I have no idea if anything bad has ever happened to Carly. I don't know. And I don't know if that's a good thing."

"Has anything bad ever happened to *you?*" In an instant the camaraderie is gone. She asks not out of worry but of defensiveness, of fear that she has failed. Her first family evaporated; this is the one that counts. The kitchen smells of desperation.

"No." And it's true: nothing that couldn't be fixed or got over, and the same for Carly, as far she knows. No husbands, no children, no death, nothing that might stain. All I carry is the quiet of this house, the slip of a door behind me.

"Then you're lucky," she says. "You're both lucky. And you should take care of each other, though I don't know how you can do that so far away."

We stand on either end of the clean kitchen floor. Behind me is the hallway, the steps upstairs, and in front the door with the flower pot holding it open, the back yard, the alley. I look at my mother and see an eighteen-year-old girl in a house I've never seen with white socks and a pegged skirt, polished nails and a tiny diamond glittering weak in the late sun, three months of this, four, six, before going back to sleep in the bed in her parents' house, ten years of sleep. My childhood bed is above me, my grown-up clothes laid out on it, waiting; two days behind me is what passes for my house, neat square rooms shut tight, a box that my family has never seen. We face each other, my mother and I, whatever might pass for *bad* locked safe in other places. Here, we are both in one piece.

———

"Look at you," my father says, hugging me. "All dolled up."

"We both are." I nod at Carly, who's drying lettuce leaves. She's in a neat white T-shirt and khaki skirt. It's something Louise would wear, but on Carly it's close to elegant. "You should have pearls on," I tell her.

She shrugs, distracted, patting the lettuce between paper towels and tossing it into a wooden bowl. Leaves litter the floor around her. It's almost seven. "I'm just going to get sauce all over myself anyway."

"Did you win?" I say to my father.

"Lost twenty bucks. You should come with me next week, be my charm."

"Martha, would you light the candles, please," my mother says, scrupulously polite. "Matches are in the towel drawer." I know this, but I don't say a word. She hasn't looked at me since I came back downstairs. Carly's eyes are on the alley, she's shaking the water from her hands, and when she reaches for the towel I see him, one hand opening the gate and the other carrying a paper bag, his hair slightly shorter but otherwise no different. There's a bottle of wine in the bag, my heels are high and my lipstick is red—this is a story I used to know.

"Why doesn't anyone ever use the front door?" I say, but she's out of the kitchen already. I light the candles and when I turn to put the matches back my mother is waiting to take them from me, her little girl, her big girl, the one she didn't need to worry about. Nothing bad will happen.

———

I'm on my third glass of wine and we're only halfway through the pasta. Carly is relaxed, effusive; my father and Edward split their attention between her and each other. Only my mother is quiet, and when I reach for the bottle again she clears her throat, refolds the napkin in her lap.

"The sauce is wonderful," I say, and fill my glass halfway.

"We wanted to get some crabs and steam them here," Carly says, "but they were still too small. You should've waited a few weeks to come up."

"What took you south, Martha?" Edward says.

"I managed a jewelry store up here, out at White Marsh. The owner wanted to open one near the Gulf Coast and needed someone to run it." The same thing I told him almost a year ago—if he'd given me a chance last night I would've told him something different, something truer.

"Do you like it?" he says.

"I'm good at it."

"How's business?" my father says. "You get much money down there?"

"Comes and goes. Not as much as here. Christmas was better than I thought it would be." I spear a few penne with my fork.

"So do you think you'll stay? Buy it out?" Edward says.

I put the fork down and lift my glass. "I haven't decided yet."

"You should eat more," my mother says softly. Her head is down, her shoulders tensed.

"You're coming up for graduation, right?" Carly dabs her lips with a napkin. Her shirt is pristine. "End of August. I was thinking a big party, inside, outside, all over the place. I'll even let you bring someone, Marth."

"Are you seeing anyone?" Edward says. My mother gets up to arrange the chicken on a serving dish. Carly's smile falters—he doesn't know me well enough to ask that question, and it fills the air like poison.

"Actually, I am." I turn to my father. "His name's Wesley. He's a guidance counselor, if you can believe that." I hold out my empty glass and he reaches behind him to the card table, picks up a new bottle and pours.

"You're kidding," Carly says. "What's he like?"

My mother brings the platter to the table and begins to clear the pasta dishes away. "You never mentioned him."

"He works at a high school in town. He's from St. Louis but he's been there a while." My father takes my hand and squeezes it. "He took me out to a carnival on the coast," I tell him. The words spill out. "Ferris wheel and all. Except I think the Baptists run it."

"No bingo?" my father says.

"No bingo." I lean back in my chair and my mother passes clean plates around.

"Would you get the salad, Martha?" she says.

"I don't know how you walk in those shoes," Carly says. "I'd fall off."

"He doesn't do academic counseling—he does the personal stuff, family problems, boyfriend problems, substance abuse." I hand the salad bowl to my father, pick a leaf from the top and pop it in my mouth.

"We didn't even *have* that," Carly says. "We had Sister Ursula—remember, Marth? 'Are you taking care of your spiritual life?'" She laughs and leans into Edward. "It was crazy. She had this drawer full of rosaries and if she really liked you she'd give you one."

I sit down and it takes a minute for the room to settle around me.

"Is it serious?" my mother says.

I shrug. "Don't know yet. We see each other on weekends." *We did—when his wife was out of town. Her name is Pamela. I never met her but that's not to say I never will—it's not easy to hide there.* "So. We . . . we go dancing," I say, and smile, glance around the table. "We go to a place up the highway and have dinner and dance."

"Since when do you dance?" Carly says. Her chicken is dismembered on her plate. She's working at the last of a thigh with her knife and fork. "I thought you liked to just sit around and look *enticing*."

I look at her, her clear forehead slightly furrowed with the effort of cutting, pale hair drawn back neat in a clip, the glint of her earrings. Our mother had her ears pierced before she could talk, swabbed the fresh holes every night before putting her in her crib, bought tiny gold hearts and chips of coral for birthdays. When my sister was old enough she took the earrings out and put them in the jewelry box on our dresser, the spinning ballerina on top long since broken.

I say nothing. The room is chilly with the sun gone and the oven turned off. Forks and knives clink. This is all we are capable of; we are exhausted by the effort it took to get this far. Carly keeps her eyes focused on her plate and my mother stares into the middle distance; Edward's face is drawn with the work of looking everywhere but at me. My father is the only one who seems content. He lays his fork down, finishes the last of his wine and smiles. He will get up and kiss my mother on the top of her head, go to the couch with the newspaper and fall asleep. His children are home. He does not know how to imagine what their lives might be like in his absence but in this house even their silence is a comfort, and if this is a mystery to him he is used to it, his wife has made him so with her sure hands and close mouth, her dogged allegiance to this family, her second, her last. Daughter, wife, mother—he is waiting for us to transform ourselves, smiling, impassive, a slow dance through the inexorable progression from one to the next. *Since when do you dance?* If I could I would fold myself in his arms and beg forgiveness. *Bless me Father, for I have sinned.*

———

The floor of our bedroom is covered with suitcases, bags, rumpled clothing, the dresser strewn with travel-size products. The air smells warm, alive, and I open the window over my bed.

"Like we never left, huh?" Carly says. She comes in and closes the door behind her, unclips her hair and begins to brush it.

I'm on the bed, shoes off. I light a cigarette and dangle it out the window.

"I thought you quit."

"I did. Special occasions."

She shimmies out of her skirt and opens a pair of neatly folded jeans with a snap of the wrist. She's still thin, as thin as she was at sixteen, her hips narrow, legs tight. "We're going out for a while. You want to come?"

I flick ashes down into the back yard. "I'm tired. Long drive."

"So what do you think?"

"I think he seems nice enough," I say. She reclips her hair and reaches up under her shirt to put deodorant on before tucking it in. "I think he's a lot older than you, and I think you're fucking him." I drag off the cigarette and tap, tap it into the dark. "I think you should be careful."

She threads a belt through the loops and stabs the point of the buckle home. "Anything else?"

I think you know exactly what else. I think that years of not talking have made it too easy for all of us to hear what isn't said. But I think if you asked me the one thing you didn't want to know for sure I'd lie to you and you'd believe me and that would be the end of it. It would be over. Ask me. Ask me and I can put it away.

I crush the cigarette out on the lip of the sill and raise my hands, palms to the ceiling. "Carly, you're a big girl. We've hardly seen each other the past few years. Why does it matter what I think? You're happy, right? You like him, Mom and Dad like him, everything's fine. What else do you want me to say?"

"You could say *you're* happy. For me, I mean. For starters. I don't need your *advice*, Martha. I don't think you're one to be giving it out anyway."

"Fair enough." I'm too tired to fight. I stand and brush ashes off my pants. "I'm going down to say good-night. There's perfume in my bag if you want some." Edward is downstairs, waiting for her. For a minute I think she'll follow me, but she doesn't move. I close the door behind me and wait for a minute, listening to the sound of her unzipping the bag, fingers moving through what I brought with me.

———

"Are you going with them?" my father says, his eyes on the television. I lean to kiss his head.

"Nope. I'm staying here with the old folks."

Edward and my mother are still at the kitchen table. It's cleared and sponged off, bare except for their glasses. I sit down at the far end and prop my feet on an empty chair.

"Where are your shoes?" my mother says.

"Upstairs. I just came down to say good-night. And nice meeting you." I nod at Edward, and my mother slides her glass to me.

"Here. You take it. I was just being sociable."

"Thanks," I say, but she doesn't look at me.

"Can I get you two anything?" she says, poised to stand. Edward and I shake our heads, and I lift the glass to drink but my eyes are blurring over, treacherous. *You two.* This is not a hotel room. It is not Wytheville or Brussels or the moon, it is nowhere safe. I tilt my head back and breathe. Edward is silent. My mother regards us both.

"It's been a long night," she says. "Don't keep her out too late."

"I won't," Edward says.

She takes her glasses off and rubs at her face, nods from behind her hands. Her fingers are swollen; her wedding band sunk deep in the flesh. I can hear Carly on the stairs.

"Okay," she says from behind me. "All set." Her smile is tight. She shoulders her purse and we all stand. She doesn't look at me and when our mother reaches for her she stiffens, accepts a kiss on the cheek and moves to take Edward's hand. He closes his eyes for an instant. The smell of my perfume fills the kitchen.

"Have a good time," my mother says, and they're gone, moving fast down the walk to the alley.

"Where are my girls?" my father yells.

"In here. We'll be in in a minute." But my mother sits down again and I do the same. She pulls Edward's glass toward her and pours more wine into it, slides the bottle to me. "When I was Carly's age I was living with my parents again," she says. "When I was your age I was engaged to your father. And I still have no idea how I got from one place to the next."

I know enough to be still, to not ask any questions. She knows the same of me.

"I didn't think I would ever have kids. I thought I'd given that up when I went back home. But I prayed and prayed and here you are, both of you. And your father. And I have no complaints." She drinks, then rubs at a drop of wine on the clean table. "You think Carly was the only one I worried about," she says, and waits, watching me.

"When we were younger—"

"When you were younger all I saw was how much you *wanted*. I worried about *that*—I didn't worry about those damn silly boys you dragged through here." She lifts her hands in frustration. "Jesus, Martha, you had no *patience*, you ran through them like—like—I don't know what. What was wrong with them?"

"Nothing," I say. "Nothing. I wasn't the one who thought anything was wrong with them, Carly—"

"Carly," she says, and slaps her hands flat on the table. "Carly didn't know what to think. She still doesn't, and that's the problem. And you—"

"What? What's wrong with me? What should I have done?"

"You should have been more generous," she says, and smiles, but her smile is miles away, years away. "Your father and I . . . we're lucky. *I'm* lucky. You never learned, Martha. You never learned to just sit back and wait for what might happen to you."

"How can you say that? I was here, I was here for thirty years—"

She shakes her head. "No. You weren't."

We sit, and the sound of the television in the next room flares and wanes. Other than that the house is quiet, no creaks or groans, every floorboard long since settled. Carly and Edward are sitting by now in whatever place they've gone to. He's tossed his pack of cigarettes on the table and holds one unlit, waiting for his drink, a foot tapping light to the music.

My mother stands and picks up the empty glasses to take to the sink. The rest of the dishes are stacked in the drainer, the pots and pans drying on the stove, the towel folded on the counter. She's touched every inch of this house more times than she could count, polished and scrubbed and shined away the possibility of anyplace else.

"I'm not asking you to come back," she says. "That's not what this is about. I'm just trying to understand what it is you *want.* I've never asked you to do anything you didn't want to do, have I? I let you go exactly where you wanted and it always seemed to be away from us. From me," she says.

If I closed my eyes and walked out the door I could find my way to the school, the church, the houses of everyone here— there are so few houses I've never been in on these blocks. I could circle the park, lay my hands on the benches there, the people who've been sitting on them for ten years, twenty, fifty. *What made you decide to move here?* I said to Edward when I met him. *It's not a place you come to and it's not a place you leave.*

"I'm sorry if it seemed that way," I say. "It wasn't."

"Then what was it? Because I'm trying here, Martha. It might be late but I'm trying."

"Let me ask you something," I say. "When you were married the first time, where did you live?" She leans heavily against the sink, looks out the window as though to make sure no one's there. "I don't want to know anything personal. Just that."

"The other side of Eastern Avenue. A few blocks east of Highland. Does that make a difference?"

I slide the wine glass back and forth on the table, sloshing what's left inside. "No difference. I was just wondering."

Why is this a secret? What mistake, what grief you couldn't have told me, that would have turned you to dust if you'd spoken it? At eighteen it's all practice, every boy, every smile, and if you fall you only break a little, if you break at all. Because after that is a whole other life, your real one, the one you couldn't see yet at eighteen but there nonetheless, Christmas trees and birthday parties and wading pools, anniversaries and lunch boxes, this house and the people in it.

"Anything else?" she says. I shake my head. "Then let me ask *you* something. What do you intend to say to your sister?"

I stand and push the chair back into place. They're on their second round, or third; if she leans in to whisper he'll smell what's left of my perfume, pale as memory. "Nothing," I say. "Not a thing."

We each have our secrets now.

T HIS IS HOW TO KEEP a secret.

Kiss your tired mother good-night, that lovely girl you never knew, frail wrists and smooth skin. Her hands may be different now but her touch has not changed. Her eyes are as green as yours. Walk past your sleeping father and crawl into your bed, narrow and sagging, and listen for voices below, the chink of the opening gate and steps on the concrete walk. Don't open your eyes—there is nothing outside you want to see.

Dream of boys, the ones you used to know: awkward, too tall, rude speech and raw hearts. When they held your hand their grip was wet with hope and misery all at once, twined together through your fingers.

I want, I want, they said.

What?

You know.

Dream of their hands, clumsy, too fast, but honest—is there anything more honest than a boy's hands?—their chewed nails and rough palms; certain of what they wanted even when their deep voices were too new to speak it. Those hands surrounded you and what they held was all the world they knew—or didn't, depending. So you chose carefully. You chose the safe ones, the ones too meek or too surprised to ask for more than what you gave them, and to some of these you gave more than what they'd ever dreamed of asking, because what harm could have come of it, what damage?

In church on Sunday you passed them on the way to Communion, their honest hands folded on the pew in front of them. You looked straight ahead, to God. One time only, a gift.

Dream of Sunday mornings, a pale dress pulled from the back of the closet and over your head, the clothes from Saturday night kicked under the bed, frayed faded denim and cork-soled sandals and rainbow tank tops smelling of spilled beer and smoke and watermelon candy. Your sister went through them while you were in the bathroom, as though she might find something wonderful there, something magic. And there was.

These boys are husbands now, sleeping on couches like your father, dreaming their own dreams while the television sings to them, or in beds with their wives, girls like you when you knew them. Their hands are not so quick anymore, the urgency gone. Nothing will disappear from under them, no one will vanish at dawn. In sleep a hand might rest on a wife's shoulder and stay there, unmoving. Their clothes are tossed on chairs in corners or hung neatly in pine-scented closets, no leaves or grass caught in cuffs or pockets, no earth ground into denim. If you saw these boys now you would weep to see what's been traded, been lost.

And if you saw their wives you would duck away, ashamed by your inadequacy, your arrogance—which is it? Which did you feel when you sat in the back of the classroom, watching them spin their hair around ink-stained fingers, chipped pink polish on filed nails? Those hands were as full of lies as the boys' were empty of them—they promised more than they gave, and what little they gave was provisional. What they wanted was an even exchange: their parents' house for their husband's, one kind of safety for another. And you, you looked around the classroom at all the boys you'd ever known and though you loved them at that moment, you knew that moment was a small one. So no exchanges, no promises, no lies, no bargaining for hearts too new to keep; just the gifts you gave, unconditional.

This was not a mistake. Remember this when your sister eases the door open and balances first on one foot and then the other to take off her clothes and slide into the bed next to yours. Remember this when you listen for the sound of his car pulling away from her, from you. You have not failed at anything that matters. This is still practice, even now—you would tell your mother this if she were to ask you, and say it in a way that both of you would believe.

The house is filled with sleep. It would be so easy to pad downstairs, take the car keys from their hook and slip out the front door no one uses, ease the car from its spot down the block and drive. His light would still be on.

But you are not about to make a mistake of this magnitude. You are old enough to know better. You are old enough to know that some secrets are worth keeping. You are old enough to realize that what is lost will eventually seem as small as the classroom you sat in fifteen years ago, waiting for the day to be over, the year, with no idea of what you might want to happen then.

Because what you understand is this: if your mother had spoken of that first husband with too much grief you would have thought that you were not the children she wanted, you were only the children she got—second chance, second choice, no difference big enough to matter. You would have believed that she could disappear from your father as quickly as you disappeared from the boys you loved only for as long as their hands were stars, daubing your skin with light; as quickly as you disappeared from the house your sister has no doubt been in tonight. This was your mistake, one that your mother would understand even better than you do. But it is a mistake that you can seal up and leave in a suitable dark, and you will. You will seal it in the dark of riddles: the noisy girls who fold into silence over cribs and stoves and dining room tables, their faces blurring with every year of happiness; the lovely boys who slide into an endless waking sleep, hands blunted and dull and empty; the houses that hold them fast.

First comes love, then comes marriage—the tune is familiar enough to be deadly. Then again, every day is deadly; every day eats away a small piece of the world that is left to you, but you move through it anyway because it's all you know to do.

Sweet girl, your mother used to say, until you were old enough to make yourself even sweeter than she knew: perfume, stolen lipstick, cheap silky underwear. You gobbled time like candy, like death. You've been keeping secrets for a long time—what's one more?

There's not room in me to keep it.

There is. Leave the boys to their sleep, stilled hands folded, eyes pressed shut. They are not yours. Leave them where they've chosen to be. Leave the girls with their husbands. You could reach a hand right through them, the path of least resistance. They have nothing to do with you.

I want.

You do. But you do not want this. You do not want what you've been taught to want, and isn't this the secret you've been keeping for longer than any of them? Isn't this the thing you've never said? Then say it now. Throw the sheets back and crawl into your sister's bed, fold her in your arms, whisper in her ear. She will struggle awake; she will want you to be someone else, but you are as close to him as she can be at this moment. Whisper her life to her, the life she's been patient enough to wait for, your mother's good girl, nothing like you. Speak to her in his voice, touch her with his hands; she will strain to hear you but sleep will suck her back down and you will leave her to its depths. Leave her to dream of her silent house, the bed that's waiting for her and the husband in it, his eyes falling shut already.

Leave them there for now. You will write, your pen dangerous as a needle, to tell them you want to visit, to come. You want. He'll open the door for you, this man who almost happened to you once, this bright ghost; he'll open a bottle of wine. And when your sister gets up to make dinner you and he will sit across the room from one another, waiting. Everything is practice but all of it counts, and none of it is over.

The three of you will eat, and drink, and when the night is over they will climb the stairs to their bed, hot and choked with the breath of years.

Sweet girl, you would drown in such a bed.